JOHN MARSHALL

SUCCESS IS A GOD IDEA

Success Is a God Idea
© 2004 by John Marshall

ISBN 0-9740693-6-1
Printed in USA

First Printing May 2004
Second Printing June 2004

All rights reserved. No part of this book may be reproduced, stored in a retrieval system, or transmitted in any form or by any means without expressed written permission of the author.

Unless otherwise noted, Scripture verses are taken from the New American Standard Bible®, Copyright © 1960, 1962, 1963, 1968, 1971, 1972, 1973, 1975, 1977, 1995 by The Lockman Foundation. Used by permission. (www.lockman.org)

Scripture verses marked NIV taken from the HOLY BIBLE, NEW INTERNATIONAL VERSION®. NIV®. Copyright © 1973, 1978, 1984 by International Bible Society. All rights reserved.

John Marshall Enterprises
P.O. Box 159
Stone Mountain, Georgia 30086
(404) 286-1139
www.johnmarshallenterprises.com
jdm@johnmarshallenterprises.com

Cover design and layout: Cathleen Kwas

DEDICATION

I dedicate this book to my compelling friend, Kenneth Gilmore, Sr., who has cheered, coached, and ever coerced me to become a writer. He constantly challenges me to greater heights, adds value to my life, and increases my contribution to the world.

Ken has stretched his intellectual acuteness by reading something on just about everything imaginable. He has the unique ability to dissect different and divergent concepts and present them in a most provocative fashion.

Ollie Mae Gilmore, Ken's mother, instilled within him an undying love for the church of Christ. May God forever use her investment in Ken and his investment in the Kingdom to further His purposes all over the world.

ACKNOWLEDGMENTS

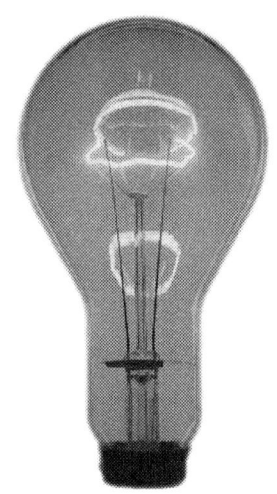

My thanks go to:

My God, who has given me the courage to write this book

My family, who has allowed me the time to do so

My number one theological discussion partner, Rachel Robertson, who has provided theological insights

My editor, Diana Scimone of Peapod Publishing, who has provided grammatical insights

My graphic designer, Cathleen Kwas, who has draped this production in the cover of greatness

TABLE OF CONTENTS

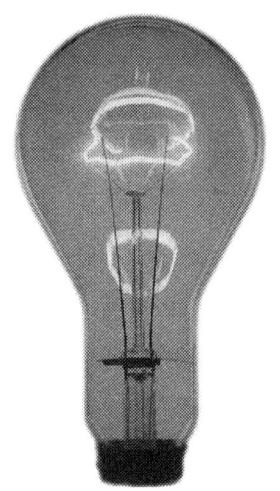

Preface.. xi
Chapter 1—What Is Success?......................... 1
Chapter 2—Success and Sacrifice 13
Chapter 3—Accomplishments of Sacrifice 27
Chapter 4—Sacrifice Leads to Success in
    All Areas of Life................................. 37
Chapter 5—Fundamentals of Sacrifice 49
Chapter 6—Persecution Grows in the Soil of Success ... 57
Chapter 7—Successfully Resisting Peer Pressure........ 71
Chapter 8—Successfully Resisting Opposition 81
Chapter 9—Successfully Forgiving.................... 91
Chapter 10—Successfully Changing 111
Chapter 11—Successfully Charging Beyond Our Past .. 119
Chapter 12—Successfully Persuading Unbelievers
    to Believe.. 127
Chapter 13—You Can Be a Success! 135

PREFACE

Many have written good books about success. So why another book on success? Why *Success Is a God Idea?*

God has granted to each of us unique experiences. Those unique experiences have helped to shape our perspectives differently; therefore, each person has a personal experienced perspective. I believe that each person should tell his or her experienced perspective. Each person has a success perspective, also, and should tell his or her success perspective. No two people are exactly alike; therefore, no two success perspectives are exactly alike.

To the extent that I am different and my experiences are different, my success perspective is different. However, *Success Is a God Idea* is really not about me. Neither is it about a health and wealth that eludes the masses. *Success Is a God Idea* is not a feel-good, name-it-and-claim-it showpiece. *Success Is a God Idea* is more about *being* successful rather than *doing* successful things. It is about God's perspective of success that He has given us so that we might experience and observe.

For me, with me, and through me, God has performed some awesome feats. He has given me the privilege to recline at ringside while He has corralled His foes, and to stand in the stadium while He has championed His friends. How great and awesome is a God like this.

I have written this book because the longer I live the more I appreciate fundamental principles that bring about real success. The older I become, the more I discover the need to teach and emphasize these principles.

Far too many in this generation have "excused" themselves from the challenge to succeed. They would rather surrender and not attempt, than fight and possibly lose. They exercise ready mental recall of their deficiencies, but seem to have little or no knowledge of His sufficiency. I prefer—and I hope that you do, as well—to trust as the apostle Paul did: "For this reason I also suffer these things, but I am not ashamed; for I know whom I have believed and I am convinced that He is able to guard what I have entrusted to Him until that day" (2 Timothy 1:12). To Him be the glory and honor.

The title of this book indicates that success proceeds from the mind of God. Indeed God does empower His people to succeed; therefore, each person should seek to succeed. For

PREFACE

those who are sincere at heart, *Success Is a God Idea* is worth the wait (reading time) and the weight (purchase price). The pages you are about to read will take you to the valley of despair and show you success there. They will take you to the mountaintop and show you success there. They will take you to the norms of everyday living and show you success there. Now take. Read.

John Marshall
May 2004

Chapter 1

WHAT IS SUCCESS?

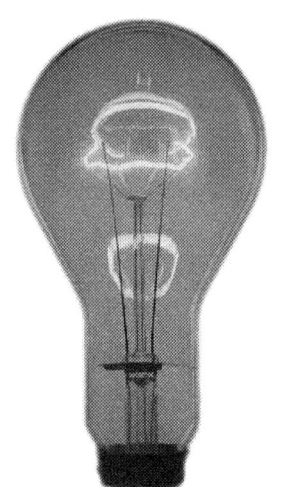

Many people define success solely as the attainment of power, prestige, position, popularity, possessions, or pleasures—or all of the above. Bookstores are filled with thousands of volumes attempting to convince others to adopt a certain lifestyle that will lead toward success. Offers for self-help sales kits make up a good portion of the mail carried by the U. S. Postal Service, FedEx, and UPS. Newspapers and magazines are filled with full-page ads offering to teach us (for a high fee) how to be successful. They promise the wealth, prestige, power, homes, stock portfolios, and everything else by which they define success.

But are these really indicators of success? Some of the most miserable and depleted people on earth have achieved one or more of these accolades. Figures throughout history such as Alexander the Great, Julius Caesar, and Napoleon lived lives of power and position, yet died broken and empty. In his book *Talking Straight*, Lee Iacocca, former chairman of Chrysler, identified our human malady when he said, "Here I am in the twilight years of my life, still wondering what it's all about…I can tell you this, fame and fortune is for the birds."[1]

Some say that true success encapsulates social, economic, and spiritual health. Abraham Maslow's theory of our "hierarchy of needs" states that success involves building blocks, and that once our basic physiological, security, belonging, and esteem needs are met, we become free to achieve our true and actual best self.

This formula is a popular one, yet is devoid of any concept of dedication to God. Can there be real success in the absence of dedication to God? Can we be successful apart from His formula for success? God planted success in the ground of our lives—and it is watered by speaking, meditating upon, and obeying His Word.

This book of the law shall not depart from your mouth, but you shall meditate on it day and night, so that you may be careful to do according to all that is written in it; for then you will make your way prosperous, and then you will have success (Joshua 1:8).

There are countless definitions for success, but for our purposes we will define it as the "healthy progression toward a predetermined wholesome goal, or the healthy progression away from an unwholesome environment." That, of course, cannot happen without God. Healthy progression marches to the cadence called out by the word of God. Success has to do with knowing and doing the will of God to the enjoyment of a favorable, satisfactory outcome.

God has an ideal will and desires for all to know His will. "This is good and acceptable in the sight of God our Savior, who desires all men to be saved and to come to the knowledge of the truth" (1 Timothy 2:3-4). We may zealously pursue education, power, and money, but they are nothing unless we remember the words of the Lord:

> Thus says the Lord, "Let not a wise man boast of his wisdom, and let not the mighty man boast of his might, let not a rich man boast of his riches; but let him who boasts boast of this, that he understands and knows Me, that I am the Lord who exercises lovingkindness, justice and righteousness on earth; for I delight in these things," declares the Lord (Jeremiah 9:23-24).

This, my friend, leads to real success. God not only wants us to be successful (remember that success is His idea), but He gives us all the tools we need to insure that we are. He wants us to believe in the resurrection of Jesus, repent of sin, confess our faith in the resurrected Jesus, and be baptized for the forgiveness of our sins. After we have been baptized, God wants us to learn His Kingdom principles. Obeying Kingdom principles enables us to live the life of faith (see Matthew 28:18-20 and James 1:22).

SUCCEED SOCIALLY

God created us to be social. He provided Adam with Eve because it was not good for him to be alone (see Genesis 2:18). Being social has to do with relating to one another. Because God wants us to be successful in our social life, through numerous "one another" passages in Scripture He has amply provided for our healthy social progression. Within the book of Romans alone, He teaches believers to:

1. Be devoted to one another (see Romans 12:10).

2. Give preference to one another (see Romans 12:10).

3. Be of the same mind toward one another (see Romans 12:16 and 15:5).

4. Love one another (see Romans 13:8).

5. Not judge one another (see Romans 14:13).

6. Pursue the things that make for peace and build up one another (see Romans 14:19)

7. Accept one another (see Romans 15:7).

8. Admonish one another (see Romans 15:14).

9. Greet one another with a holy kiss (see Romans 16:16).

Believers within the first-century church clearly understood that God created them for "one anotherness" relationships. They devoted themselves to fellowship, home visitations, and sharing all they owned—and God prospered them. God's purpose has not changed; twenty centuries later, He still desires that His people succeed socially—and there can be no doubt that He guides us toward social success.

SUCCEED ECONOMICALLY

In His parables, Jesus frequently spoke about money (see Matthew 18:21-35, Matthew 19:16-26, Matthew 25:14-25, Luke 7:41-43, and Luke 10:25-37). God is well aware of economics. He wants His people to be successful economically. Therefore, He provided for their economic advancement. Such wealthy warriors of the faith as Abraham, Solomon, and Lydia greatly advanced God's agenda. Heroic men and women of God enjoyed economic success and understood that it came by the hand of God. The psalmist said it best when he declared that God does not withhold any good thing from those who walk uprightly (see Psalm 84:11). Throughout the Scriptures, God gives us wisdom on how to succeed economically in passages such as 1 Kings 3:13, 1 Chronicles 29:28, 2

Chronicles 17:5, 2 Chronicles 32:27, and Proverbs 22:4.

SUCCEED SPIRITUALLY

While God enables us to experience economic success, He also desires for us to succeed spiritually. Consider the Israelites according to Deuteronomy chapter 8. The hand of God delivered to them unparalleled economic success. The promised land provided wealth and prosperity galore. Even God described it as "a land flowing with milk and honey" (Exodus 3:8)—but God saw a need to warn them of becoming spiritually lethargic. He warned them of self-induced amnesia, yet they ignored His warnings, bringing calamity after calamity upon themselves.

God does desire for us to succeed in every area of our lives, but danger lurks beyond success for those who ignore their spiritual success. Spiritual success has to do with what proceeds from the mind of God. Amazingly, God gave us the ability to know what is on His mind, and in fact to actually have the mind of Christ.

> Now we have received, not the spirit of the world, but the Spirit who is from God, so that we may know the things freely given to us by God, which things we also speak, not in words taught by human wisdom, but in those taught by the Spirit, combining spiritual thoughts with spiritual words.

> But a natural man does not accept the things of the Spirit of God, for they are foolishness to him; and he cannot understand them, because they are spiritually appraised. But he who is spiritual appraises all things, yet he himself is appraised by no one. For who has known the mind of the Lord, that he will instruct Him? But we have the mind of Christ (1 Corinthians 2:12-16).

Success is a God idea. Given that the idea of success proceeded from the mind of God, success must also be a good idea. God has always spoken and acted with the goal of accomplishing His whole healthy objective. And He has always empowered His people to accomplish it. We can look at three different eras of the history of God's people in order to prove this point.

SUCCESS DURING THE PATRIARCHAL DISPENSATION

Success during the patriarchal dispensation was a God idea. During these years, God intentionally promoted the social, economic, and spiritual well-being of His people. He blessed the patriarchs. To be blessed was to be positioned for prosperity. To be positioned for prosperity was to have people and circumstances synchronized and favorably aligned for one's benefit.

Look at the life of Abraham, for example. After the death

of his wife, Sarah, Abraham sought a wife for his son Isaac. He sent one of his servants to his country and to search among his relatives for a wife for Isaac. The servant faithfully went about his task even invoking the help of God: "O Lord, the God of my master Abraham, please grant me success today, and show lovingkindness to my master Abraham" (Genesis 24:12). God granted him success, and the servant discovered Rebekah, who willingly followed the servant and became a wife for Isaac. On behalf of Abraham, God granted success to his servant.

SUCCESS DURING THE MOSAIC DISPENSATION

By the time of Moses, success had become a proven principle of God. He promised success to His people, and He delivered. To Moses' successor, Joshua, God promised success and provided His formula to assure it:

> Only be strong and very courageous; be careful to do according to all the law which Moses My servant commanded you; do not turn from it to the right or to the left, so that you may have success wherever you go. This book of the law shall not depart from your mouth, but you shall meditate on it day and night, so that you may be careful to do according to all that is written in it; for then you will make your way prosperous, and then you will have success (Joshua 1:7-8).

Throughout the Old Testament, the people of God lived with the hope of success, and God granted it to them, intentionally promoting the social, economical, spiritual well-being of His people. King David believed that God would provide success for his son Solomon. "Now, my son, the Lord be with you that you may be successful, and build the house of the Lord your God just as He has spoken concerning you" (1 Chronicles 22:11). Nehemiah prayed for success, "O Lord, I beseech You, may Your ear be attentive to the prayer of Your servant and the prayer of Your servants who delight to revere Your name, and make Your servant successful today and grant him compassion before this man" (Nehemiah 1:11).

SUCCESS DURING THE CHRISTIAN DISPENSATION

Jesus shared His desire for believers to live a successful life: "The thief comes only to steal and kill and destroy; I came that they may have life, and have it abundantly" (John 10:10). This is not a life of barely hanging on or merely existing. The people of God should never hang on, but rather be strong in the Lord and in His mighty power (see Ephesians 6:10-17). This is passionate, purposeful living that compels and propels people toward God.

Jesus sent His disciples to evangelize the world, telling them to baptize those who would believe. Baptism would indicate that they were successful in their efforts to convince non-believers of the truth that Jesus was Lord. Yes, Jesus intended for His disciples to successfully persuade unbelievers to believe. Confidently, He commissioned His disciples to traverse the entire world and lead people to Him—and He outlined the way they could successfully fulfill this commission: "You will receive power when the Holy Spirit has come upon you; and you shall be My witnesses both in Jerusalem, and in all Judea and Samaria, and even to the remotest part of the earth" (Acts 1:8).

We are still living in the Christian dispensation, and God still desires to grant success to His people. He is still intentionally promoting the social, economic, and spiritual well-being of His people. God still wants believers to prosper in all areas of life just as their soul prospers (see 3 John 1:2).

The apostles and prophets knew precisely and exactly the mind of God (see Ephesians 3:5). God wants all believers to be successful spiritually. The question is not whether God has promised us success. His Word shows that He has:

> "For I know the plans that I have for you," declares the Lord, "plans for welfare and not for calamity to give you a future and a hope. Then you will call upon Me and come and pray to Me, and I will listen to you. You will seek Me and find Me when you search for Me with all your heart" (Jeremiah 29:11-13).

The question is, will we accept His definition of success, and will we do what He requires in order to bring about that success in our lives?

Is the Holy Spirit stirring your heart? Is He showing you that some of the things you have pursued in your life—even in good faith—do not line up with His definition of success, or the success that He has planned for you since the beginning of the ages? In the rest of this book, we will attempt to smooth the often-rough road that leads to success. We will study God's principles that undergird success, and see how to appropriate the success that He provides.

THOUGHT PROVOKERS

1. How have you defined success in the past? How do you now define success? How has your understanding improved?

2. How will this knowledge empower you to become successful?

3. How has God's desire for success differed from dispensation to dispensation?

Chapter 2

SUCCESS AND SACRIFICE

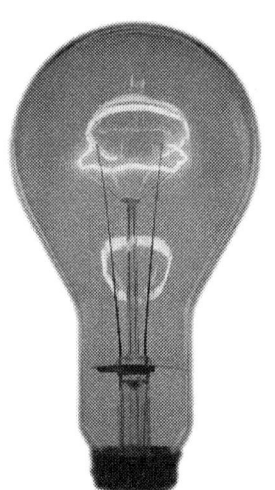

Sacrifice? What in the world does sacrifice have to do with success? Sacrifice has everything to do with success. In fact, there is no such thing as success without sacrifice. Only an immature person (or an idealistic one) would think it is possible to achieve such a reward without a cost. The word of God teaches that we reap (enjoy success) in direct proportion to what we have sown (sacrificed). "Do not be deceived, God is not mocked; for whatever a man sows, this he will also reap" (Galatians 6:7).

We have seen that throughout the patriarchal and Mosaic dispensations, and now within the Christian dispensation, God has continually granted prosperity and success to His faithful people. The attitude that accompanied each example was that of sacrifice. The best example of a sacrificial attitude is the cross. The cross was the ultimate success story, but it was also the ultimate sacrifice. For Jesus, the cross was not a decorative ornament to wear around His neck. The cross was about the expensive cost of life and death. It symbolized the depths of the ultimate sacrifice that Jesus made for us.

That is why He frequently taught His disciples about His impending death on the cross, and how sacrifice was a non-negotiable part of His purpose in life. "From that time Jesus began to show His disciples that He must go to Jerusalem, and suffer many things from the elders and chief priests and scribes, and be killed, and be raised up on the third day" (Matthew 16:21). He was about to make the ultimate sacrifice for them (and for all mankind), and in turn He required sacrifice of those who would follow after Him: "Then Jesus said to His disciples, 'If anyone wishes to come after Me, he must deny himself, and take up his cross and follow Me'" (Matthew 16:24). Jesus looked to His death on the cross with resolve and steadfastness, and He appealed to His disciples to be committed as well to the task set before them.

We all want success in our personal lives, families, and church, but our willingness to sacrifice reveals the extent of our commitment and determination. Our willingness to sacrifice indicates the strength and the level of our commitment and determination. A committed determination frequently involves sacrifice. It does not permit us to promise, "There is no mountain too high, no valley too low, no river too wide to keep me from you," when we really mean, "I will be there tonight if it does not rain." Regardless of our words, our sacrifice paints the true picture of our determination. In fact, the sacrificial price tag always attaches itself to success. We will succeed only to the extent that we willingly sacrifice for the success we desire.

There are two main types of sacrifice—self-sacrifice and substance sacrifice.

SELF-SACRIFICE

Self-sacrifice is the willingness to give of ourselves above and beyond our initial intentions. The apostle Paul alluded to self-sacrifice when he challenged the Roman saints:

> Therefore I urge you, brethren, by the mercies of God, to present your bodies a living and holy sacrifice, acceptable to God, which is your spiritual service of worship. And do not be conformed to this world, but be transformed by the renewing of your mind, so that you may prove what the will of God is, that which is good and acceptable and perfect (Romans 12:1-2).

The word *urge* in this passage is translated from the Greek word *parakleo*, which means "to call and come alongside to help." Paul urged believers to sacrifice, and he also came alongside them to help them follow his counsel. In addition, he told them that they could do this only by the "mercies of God." *Mercy* means "special and immediate regard to eliminate the misery of another." Those whom Paul counseled, God also aided to follow his counsel.

God challenges us to make a living sacrifice, too. A living sacrifice is the holy offering of our bodies to God. God accepts a holy body offered unto Him. To offer our living bodies to God, we must love Him with priority and deny self with a passion.

God challenges us to make a logical sacrifice, a spiritual service of worship. A logical sacrifice is the whole offering of our bodies to God. The word *spiritual* is *logikos,* which means "a logical and mental deliberation." Sacrifice is determined to be the proper and practical thing to do. It engages the intellect and involves the total self.

God challenges believers to change. In fact, we could call this type of self-sacrifice a "challenging sacrifice." Challenging sacrifice changes believers morally. Paul says, "Do not be conformed to this world" (Romans 12:2). To conform is to assume an outward expression that is contrary to our inner nature even though our behavior conforms to this world (this sinful age).

Challenging sacrifice also changes believers mentally. Herein lies another passive imperative solicitation of mental transformation: "Be transformed by the renewing of your mind" (Romans 12:2). To transform is to manifest outwardly complete and continual change in daily living. It is to metamorphose, as a butterfly comes to be from a larva. It is to radiate an inner glory as did Jesus in His transfiguration (see Matthew 17:2 and 2 Corinthians 3:18). When Paul says, "Be transformed by the renewing of your mind," by reason he means, "Change your mind, which will in turn change your behavior."

What a picture of self-sacrifice. First, Paul was urging believers to renew their minds. Renewed minds would take them beyond their initial intentions. Yes, a changed mind precedes changed behavior. Changed behavior requires going further than one's initial intentions. That is self-sacrifice, and to live the Christian lifestyle requires self-sacrifice. We have to do what we did not initially plan to do. From time to time, God calls us to sacrifice. He calls us to go further than we initially intended to go. If we never go beyond what we originally planned to do, we will never do much for God.

Has not there been a time when you said, "I am never going to do that. It is not worth it, and therefore I refuse to go that route"? Maybe your oldest daughter joined the junior high school band. You purchased an expensive flute for her, rearranged your work schedule to pick her up every day after band practice, and attended her performances. Three months before the end of the school year, she became disillusioned and quit the band. You declared it was a waste of time and money, and vowed you would never go through that again.

A few years later, your younger daughter wants to join the junior high school band and play the baritone saxophone. What are you going to do? You are going to do what every good parent would do: Go beyond your original intention. You vowed you would never go this route again, but you purchase another expensive musical instrument, rearrange your work schedule once again, pick up your daughter from band practice daily, and attend her performances. You make a sacrifice. Children always cause their parents to make sacrifices, to do things they never intended to do. That is the definition of self-sacrifice.

Often when we are willing to make a sacrifice, others will oppose us. When Jesus told His disciples that He was going to give His life as a sacrifice, Peter opposed Him, saying that he would not allow Jesus to make such a sacrifice. Peter did not understand the importance of Jesus' sacrifice. When Jesus mentioned His impending death, what did Peter do? He declared that he would never allow that to happen. As one of His closest disciples in the inner circle (the others were James and John), Peter experienced a close fellowship with Jesus. Jesus exposed him to and afforded him great insights, yet he failed to understand and appreciate His sacrifice.

SUBSTANCE SACRIFICE

The second type of sacrifice is substantive sacrifice, which means that we are willing to give of our substance over and beyond our original expectation. The apostle Paul alluded to substance sacrifice when he told the Corinthians of the Macedonian's giving.

> Now, brethren, we wish to make known to you the grace of God which has been given in the churches of Macedonia, that in a great ordeal of affliction their abundance of joy and their deep poverty overflowed in the wealth of their liberality. For I testify that according to their ability, and beyond their ability, they gave of their own accord, begging us with much urging for the favor of participation in the support of the saints, and this, not as we had expected, but they first gave themselves to the Lord and to us by the will of God (2 Corinthians 8:1-5).

The Macedonians were treading in deep poverty. How poor were they? Their deep poverty caused the apostle Paul to excuse them from his request to help support the other saints. He looked at them and said, "They don't have enough for themselves. Therefore, we will not burden them by asking them to give to others." Yet the Macedonians begged him for an opportunity to give, and they gave beyond the original expectation of the apostle Paul. The Macedonians were so impoverished that Paul said, "We didn't even ask them, but they came along and did better than the people we asked." Isn't that amazing? They gave beyond their ability. Out of their deep poverty, the abundance of their joy propelled them into sacrifice.

Suppose your grandmother is on a fixed income of $500 per month. You wonder how she survives each month. You notice that when she buys her groceries and pays the utility bills, she has little to nothing left. Due to poor money management, you are three months behind on your $1,500 per month mortgage. Would you ask your grandmother for financial assistance? Probably not—but why not? Because you think that she is totally unable to assist you financially. When she asks if she can help, you refuse. Even when she insists, your conscience will not allow you to take money from one whom you perceive is in such dire straits herself. Then you find out that your grandmother went to the bank and paid your entire delinquent mortgage. That is a substance sacrifice.

FRIENDS OR ENEMIES?

Usually the unspiritual and the immature will fail to understand and appreciate when someone is willing to sacrifice. During a period of immaturity, the apostle Peter failed to understand and appreciate Jesus' willingness to sacrifice:

> From that time Jesus began to show His disciples that He must go to Jerusalem, and suffer many things from the elders and chief priests and scribes, and be killed, and be raised up on

the third day. Peter took Him aside and began to rebuke Him, saying, "God forbid it, Lord! This shall never happen to You" (Matthew 16:21-22).

The people who are closest to us will often interfere with our willingness to sacrifice for the success that we desire. Even the people who frequent our religious circle may object. Immature and unspiritual church members may not understand the power of our sacrifice, and would not consider following suit. They will mock our investment, saying, "Have you lost your mind? You don't have excess to give. God doesn't want you to give or help anyone else until you have an abundance for yourself." At times like this, we must remind them of the Macedonian report in 2 Corinthians chapter 8, reiterating that it is always better to honor God before rewarding self.

Job's wife disagreed with her husband's willingness to make sacrifice. She counseled him to cut his losses and abandon God (see Job 2:9). A spiritually minded husband who is married to an unspiritually minded wife may hear her say, "We can't give that much money! Man, what's wrong with you, giving that away?" When we begin to sacrifice for the success that we desire, people who do not understand our commitment will make light of our willingness to sacrifice. They believe that our giving to God has nothing to do with our relationship with Him—but giving to God has everything to do with our relationship with Him.

Consider the rich man who had not given to poor Lazarus (see Luke chapter 16), the rich ruler who refused to sell and give to the poor (see Luke chapter 18), and Demas who allowed the goods of the world to cloud his spiritual foresight (see 2 Timothy 4:10). Remember Cain, Lot, Judas, Ananias and Sapphira, and even Achan who lusted after the loot. They thought blessings came with receiving, when Jesus said that they came with giving (see Acts 20:35). Success and sacrifice go hand in hand.

Young people who tell their classmates that they cannot talk long on the phone at night because they must study for an upcoming chemistry exam may receive laughter and mocking in reply. Their friends may fail to appreciate the sacrifice they intend to make in order to win the scholarship they desire. They neither understand nor appreciate their sacrifice needed to succeed in school.

Our immature and unspiritual friends and family members can actually become agents of the devil against our willingness to sacrifice. Is that not amazing? If it happened to Jesus, it will happen to us. When His close friend Peter rebuked Him for His willingness to make sacrifice, Jesus said, "Get behind Me, Satan!" (Matthew 16:23). Peter did not realize that he was actually working on behalf of Satan. What would have happened if Jesus had listened to Peter? Forgiveness would not be available, we would still be in our sins, and the church would be non-existent. Jesus was willing to sacrifice for the success set before Him.

Could it be that our closest friends think they are helping us when indeed they are actually causing us much harm? Could it be that *we* think our closest friends are helping us when they are actually causing us much harm? Could it be that some of our closest friends are actually agents of the devil. They are if they interfere with us when we attempt to make an appropriate sacrifice.

The maximum quality of life—or success—comes only to those who are willing to make sacrifice. Jesus said to His disciples, "If anyone wishes to come after Me, he must deny himself, and take up his cross and follow Me" (Matthew 16:24). Concentration camp survivor Corrie Ten Boom once said that she learned not to hold on to anything too tightly, because it hurt too much when God had to pry back her fingers to get to it. We, too, had better not hold on to anything too tightly, but rather live life with an open hand, letting God give and take as He pleases. Yes, we must sacrifice for quality spiritual life.

Jesus said the same thing 2,000 years earlier. "For whoever wishes to save his life will lose it; but whoever loses his life for My sake will find it" (Matthew 16:25). The maximum quality of life comes to those who willingly go above and beyond. We must learn to rebuke everyone and everything that interferes with our making sacrifices. Jesus rebuked Peter when He told him to get behind, and likewise our love for God must exceed our love for anyone and anything.

That sacrifice begins with salvation. God wants everyone to be saved, but before we can enjoy the salvation of the Lord, we must make sacrifices—we must sacrifice our way of thinking and believing that opposes God. Many will never enjoy salvation because they will never give up their thoughts about how salvation ought to come. Peter sacrificed his own way of thinking, and we see him change from a man who denied the Lord three times to someone who professed his love to Jesus and lived a life that exemplified that love.

God inspired the apostles to preach the message of salvation. They taught that through faith, repentance, and baptism, one obtained forgiveness of sins. "Peter said to them, 'Repent, and each of you be baptized" (Acts 2:38). Clearly, baptism is a required step in the process of salvation.

If your thoughts are contrary to the will of God, you must put aside your own thoughts and even your parents' thoughts. Are you willing to make that commitment in order to succeed at the tasks and dreams that God has set before you? Write down three areas in which you want to succeed. What sacrifices must you make in order to succeed? Who and what must you rebuke in order to make the necessary sacrifices?

THOUGHT PROVOKERS

1. What does someone's sacrifice tell us about his committed determination?

2. What motivates someone to sacrifice self?

3. What motivates someone to sacrifice substance?

Chapter 3

ACCOMPLISHMENTS OF SACRIFICE

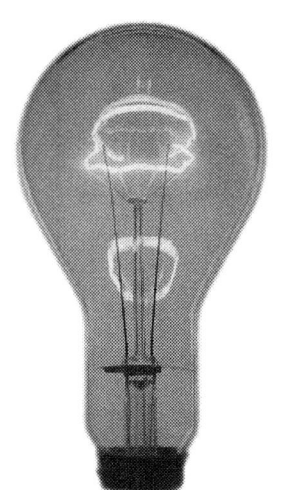

In the previous chapter, we learned that there is no success without sacrifice. We reap (or enjoy) success in direct proportion to what we have sown (or sacrificed). The reason that God expects us to sacrifice is not because He is a cruel being who enjoys watching us suffer, but rather because He knows that the benefits of sacrifice far outweigh the momentary pain we may endure.

During much of my time as a college student, I worked forty hours per week. Occasionally, on Tuesdays and Thursdays I left class at 1:20 p.m., drove to Buchanan's Exxon station, changed into my work clothes in their restroom, went around the corner to eat a quick lunch at Carroll's Rib Shack, and made it to my job at the Motor Parts and Bearing Company by 2:00 p.m.

Working until 9:00 each evening left me too exhausted to

study at night, so I had to study during the day. This forced me to develop a routine. Immediately after each class, I went to my favorite corner in the library and restudied the just-ended class. I had to learn the material each day because I did not have the time to review it to learn it later.

Every day, I gave up the opportunity to chat in the hall and sleep in the library. Every day, I missed the opportunity to lie dormant under the inviting shade of the oak trees near the lake on the campus lawn. Through that experience, I learned not just my academic lessons, but also the discipline that allowed me to remain on the dean's list. That discipline has carried me through life—the same discipline that has enabled me to write this book.

God used my sacrifice to bring an increase in my own life (leading to success in my own life) and to motivate others (leading to success in their lives)—including motivating you as you read this book. These are two important Kingdom principles concerning success, and we will look at each of them in more detail.

GOD USES OUR SACRIFICE AS A BASIS TO MOTIVATE OTHERS.

God judges the sacrifice of one person independently from the sacrifice of another person—but He uses the fact that one person sacrificed in order to motivate another. When Paul wrote to the Corinthian believers, he challenged them with the example that the Macedonians had set:

> Now, brethren, we wish to make known to you the grace of God which has been given in the churches of Macedonia, that in a great ordeal of affliction their abundance of joy and their deep poverty overflowed in the wealth of their liberality. For I testify that according to their ability, and beyond their ability, they gave of their own accord, begging us with much urging for the favor of participation in the support of the saints, and this, not as we had expected, but they first gave themselves to the Lord and to us by the will of God. So we urged Titus that as he had previously made a beginning, so he would also complete in you this gracious work as well (2 Corinthians 8:1-6).

Paul used the generosity of the Macedonians in the midst of their poverty in order to challenge and motivate the Corinthian church. The Macedonians did not pledge to give; they just gave. The Corinthians, on the other hand, had pledged a year in advance to give, but had not fulfilled their pledge. First, Paul bragged to the Macedonians about what the Corinthians had promised to do. Then, he bragged to the Corinthians about what the Macedonians had done—in an effort to motivate the Corinthians to do what they had agreed to do.

> For it is superfluous for me to write to you about this ministry to the saints; for I know your readiness, of which I boast about you to the Macedonians, namely, that Achaia has been prepared since last year, and your zeal has stirred up most of them (2 Corinthians 9:1-2).

This is a principle with which we are familiar. When we want to motivate someone, we refer to what someone else has done, is doing, or will do. As a parent, I do not hesitate to tell my children and all other students that I worked forty hours a week and stayed on the dean's list throughout college (and still enjoyed way too much goof-off time). Why do I do that? I do not tell them this to brag. In fact, I do not even consider myself to be above average. I do it because I constantly try to motivate young people to be all that they can be academically and professionally.

Whenever I encounter someone who claims that they cannot arrive on time because of their children, I quickly tell them that my wonderful wife, Priscilla, and I (mostly Priscilla) prepared three children for church every week, drove seventy-five miles from Memphis, Tennessee, to Jonesboro, Arkansas, every Sunday, and were never late.

This principle works—in the natural and in the spiritual. God uses our sacrifice to motivate others. He loves to brag on His people, to show them off, and He wants to motivate others by showing them what His people have done.

GOD USES OUR SACRIFICE AS A BASIS UPON WHICH TO MULTIPLY UNTO US.

Peter reminded Jesus of what he had sacrificed when he said, "We have left everything and followed You" (Mark 10:28). Peter really meant, "Lord, don't You forget what I gave up for You!" On the surface, this may seem like bragging or even nagging, but Peter understood that God uses our sacrifice as a basis upon which to bless us or multiply unto us. So he really was asking, "What am I going to get for what I have given up?" Observe how Jesus responded:

> Jesus said, "Truly I say to you, there is no one who has left house or brothers or sisters or mother or father or children or farms, for My sake and for the gospel's sake, but that he will receive a hundred times as much now in the present age, houses and brothers and sisters and mothers and children and farms, along with persecutions; and in the age to come, eternal life" (Mark 10:29-30).

Jesus was saying, "I am telling you, Peter, what you have sacrificed is the basis upon which I am going to multiply unto you. It is okay to have those kind of thoughts. I know human nature wants to know. So let Me answer that for you. No one has given up mother, father, sister, brother, houses, or farms, except that I will multiply and return it to him. God will bless your sacrifice."

We can feel guilty when we think about what we are going to get from God when we give up something for Him, but He is saying that it is perfectly all right to wonder. God not only understands our questions, but He even answers them.

Some will foolishly say, "I just give and expect nothing in return." That is an unspiritual idea. They might counter that Luke refuted that idea when he says, "But love your enemies, and do good, and lend, expecting nothing in return; and your reward will be great, and you will be sons of the Most High; for He Himself is kind to ungrateful and evil men" (Luke 6:35). Their argument is that Luke taught that we should expect nothing from the ones to whom we do good, but even that verse teaches that a reward comes: "Your reward will be great." Luke taught that we expect nothing from the ones to whom we do the good deed—but that God rewards us. Luke taught the same principle later in his gospel account:

> And He also went on to say to the one who had invited Him, "When you give a luncheon or a dinner, do not invite your friends or your brothers or your relatives or rich neighbors, otherwise they may also invite you in return and that will be your repayment. But when you give a reception, invite the poor, the crippled, the lame, the blind, and you will be blessed, since they do not have the means to repay you; for you will be repaid at the resurrection of the righteous" (Luke 14:12-14).

Imagine a farmer planting corn and saying, "I'm putting this seed in the ground, but I don't look for anything in return." A farmer with that outlook would not be in business long. A good farmer plants his seed in the ground and then expects a good harvest. He is actually expecting God to multiply his sacrifice. God will do that, but He can multiply only the seeds that the farmer planted. He cannot multiply what the farmer did not plant.

When we ask God to do something for us, He replies, "Come in and let's talk about it. Bring your sacrifice sheet in. Bring in the sheet with all the sacrifices you have made, and we will talk about it. I'm going to return to you on the basis that you sacrificed for Me." Note that God makes qualitative judgments, not quantitative ones; He judges our sacrifice independently based on the fact that we did sacrifice, not on how much we sacrificed.

If this still does not seem convincing, look at Mark 10:29-30 again. What did Jesus say the ones who sacrifice will receive? Why did He say they will receive it? How will they receive it? He said they will receive what they sacrificed, that is, what they gave up. They will receive because they first sacrificed, and they will receive according to their sacrifice. God uses our sacrifice as a basis to multiply unto us. When God gets ready to bless us, He looks at our sacrifice.

When the apostles responded in an unspiritual manner, Jesus did not hesitate to rebuke them (see Luke 10:17-20). So if Peter had asked an improper question, Jesus would certainly have corrected him. Since He gave an answer, not a rebuke, we must conclude that Peter asked a legitimate question.

Sacrifice is a God idea. Success is a God idea. Yes, both sacrifice and success are God ideas. Since they are His ideas, He uses them however He chooses.

Sacrifice and success are inherently connected—although it is human nature to try to separate them. Too many people want success without sacrifice. Some student athletes, for example, want success in the professional ranks, but they are unwilling to sacrifice in order to achieve that level. They have professional talents, but they will not attend class, stay out of trouble, practice, or follow the discipline set by the coaches. Achieving success takes sacrifice, but too many are not willing to pay the cost—and not just for professional athletes. No matter what job, ministry, dream, or vision that we pursue, there will be times when sacrifice is required. Sacrifice and success are inherently connected because God put them together. Therefore, if we will not make the sacrifice, our success will be minimum. We must sacrifice today in order to have success tomorrow.

Sacrifice and success are personal issues, but they are not private. If personal sacrifice was private, God would not have told the Corinthians about the Macedonians sacrifice. If personal sacrifice was private, God would not have told the Macedonians what the Corinthians had promised to do.

Sacrifice and success are open for public discussion. Only then can they motivate another.

Write the names of three people who you have motivated with your sacrifice. If you are unaware of anyone you have motivated with your sacrifice, then you probably have made inadequate sacrifices.

List three occasions when you can connect your sacrifice to the multiplication that God has returned to you. If you are unaware of an occasion when God has multiplied your sacrifice, then you probably need to pay closer attention to your blessings. You should be able to point to specific times in your life when you can say, "God, I did this for You, and now I thank You for doing this for me." Remember that God uses our sacrifice as a basis to motivate others, and He uses our sacrifice as a basis upon which to multiply unto us.

THOUGHT PROVOKERS

1. Why does God use our sacrifice to multiply unto us?

2. How much do we need to know about the sacrifice of others before we become motivated by it?

3. What risks do we take when we mention the sacrifice of others?

Chapter 4

SACRIFICE LEADS TO SUCCESS IN ALL AREAS OF LIFE

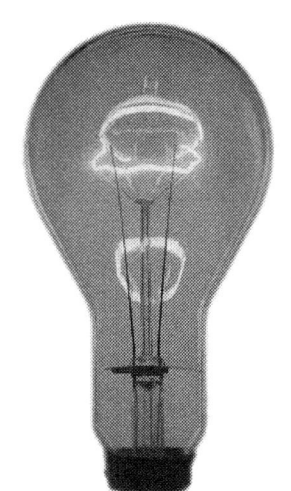

I f a farmer wants to enjoy watermelons, he will plant watermelon seeds. Through his hard work and favorable factors, the harvest becomes plentiful. This principle of sowing (sacrificing) and reaping (success) is woven into the very fabric of the universe. This becomes a valuable principle to follow in all of life. Sacrifice is designed to lead to success. God planned it that way.

SACRIFICE LEADS TO SUCCESS WITHIN THE FAMILY.

In 1991 while attending Memphis State University (now the University of Memphis), I wrote a paper for my graduate studies entitled *Single-Mothering Stimulates a Positive Family Networking Within Black Families*. Below is an excerpt from that researched conclusion. As you read it, remember that a positive statement about the Black family is not intended to be a negative statement about a non-Black family.

Blacks often attempt, through informal channels, to accomplish what non-Blacks may accomplish through formal channels. For example, Whites may formally and legally adopt neglected children, whereas, Blacks are more apt to simply care for neglected children without formally adopting them. In his 1973 study, Billingsley found that networking has been and is one of the strongest Black cultural patterns. The Black family networks to minimize housing expenses. In a recent study Hogan (1990) reported that almost one-half (44.7%) of Black single-mothers lived in the same household as did their mothers, while only 22.5% of White single-mothers lived in the same household with their mothers. Hogan also discovered that a total of 56.4% of Black single-mothers lived in a household with an adult kin, other than a husband, while only 30.6% of White single-mothers lived in the same household with an adult kin other than a husband. Hogan also discovered that overall 44% of married and/or single Black mothers lived with one or more adult kin (not husband) compared to only 11% overall for White mothers.

The Black family networks to minimize child-care expenses. Hogan (1990) found that 46% of Black mothers used grandmothers as primary child-care providers as compared to only 34%

for Whites. In many instances the grandmothers who babysit are likely to render their services free of charge.

The Black family networks to share income. Garfinkel (1986) discovered that single parents tend to have lower income, as a matter of fact two-parent families tend to have more than twice the income of single-parent families. Garfinkel further found that one out of every two single-women headed households lived under the poverty level as compared to only one out of every ten among those women who were married.

Hogan (1990) found that 19% of Black single-mothers received one-half or more of their financial support from individuals other than a spouse. Only 8% of White single-mothers received one-half or more of their support from individuals other than a spouse (Hogan).

Garfinkel (1986) concluded that Black families have access to stronger more persuasive kin networks and kin support networks and these at least partially compensate for the absence of a male earner in the Black family.

Billingsley (1973) noted that ethnographic descriptions of the Black family suggest that the mutual exchange of goods and services among Black family members benefit not only economically but psychologically. McAdoo (1978) noted that Black kins network for stress support. Billingsley also noted that Black kinship networks encourage and aid single-mothers in adapting to the stress of mothering.

Gibson (1982) investigated race and life-stages and compared national data collected in 1957 and 1976 and noticed the differences in the use of informal helpers in coping with psychological distress. Her (Gibson) analysis revealed that in coping with distress Blacks used a more diverse pool of informal family help than did Whites.

Chatters, Taylor and Neighbors (1985) confirmed this in their research for they found that Black women have a large health network and were more likely than Whites to receive support from extended family members. According to Chatters et. al., 86.9% of Black women with a personal problem reported using informal assistance, with the most utilized category of informal help being a mother followed by a sister.

According to McAdoo, the social family network acts to provide emotional support and protect the family's integrity from assaults by external forces.

Conclusion: Ethnographic descriptions of the Black family suggest that the mutual exchange and sharing of goods and services is more effectively done among Blacks than among Whites (Angel and Tienda 1982).[2]

Very likely, recent research would discover a dysfunctional difference, probably due to a failure to continue to make such sacrifices as are needed to maintain intact families of integrity. Unfortunately many indicators suggest that the Black family has to a great degree abandoned their sacrificial dynamic that helped lead to success. However, this would still argue for the fact that sacrifice leads to success within the family.

All families desire success, and all families must sacrifice to achieve that success. Often that means going "above and beyond"—above initial intentions and beyond original expectations. That starts right after the wedding. When husbands and wives discover that they did not marry the person they dated, they must then learn to make sacrifices. The person they dated was lovely and cooperative, but most people who are dating do not have a clue what marriage requires. Once they say, "I do," they quickly come to the realization that they did not marry the lovely and cooperative person they dated. In order for their marriage to succeed, they must now go above and beyond their initial intentions and expectations.

Parents must make sacrifices for their children. No one tells prospective parents that pretty little babies can be so fussy. It never crossed their mind that cute little babies can be so sick at times. They had no idea that their precious little son or daughter could get so sick and keep them awake so many hours during the night. No one told them about the sacrifices required in order to be successful at parenting.

Nor did they know that children were so costly. The bills for education and food are enormous. Parents look forward to the day when their children turn eighteen and leave home to start their own lives (and pay for it themselves)—but think again. They never leave home. They just go away and bring more people back with them.

The sacrifices, however, are not one-sided. Children must make sacrifices for their parents. What son or daughter would ever think that their sweet petite mother would become a monster when she reached age seventy-five? Who knew that she would refuse to eat her food, bathe, or change clothes? Now that she has developed Alzheimer's, she is a totally different person. Who would think that their once strong and commanding father would now need to be commanded to take his medicine? Our parents made sacrifices for us, and now we must make sacrifices for our parents.

The family is God's fundamental foundational institution. Therefore, we must go above and beyond in order to succeed within the family—and that invariably involves sacrifice.

SACRIFICE LEADS TO SUCCESS IN SCHOOL.

To be academically successful, we must willingly sacrifice to satisfy our instructors. When our children come home and say, "My teacher is so mean and demanding," we need to tell them to close their mouths, open their minds, sit in class, listen to instructions, and work hard. Hard work will not hurt them. When they work hard, they will succeed. We should not attempt to cushion them from making the necessary sacrifices.

All too often parents side with their children, and that is to their detriment. Some parents even take off work, show up at school, and cause unnecessary ruckus—defending their children rather than working with their teachers in order to help their children succeed. Will the child really suffer if he has to write a longer paper? Will she die if she has to rewrite a paper? If the child writes a better paper the second time, the parent should praise the teacher for assigning the rewrite, rather than denouncing the teacher for the extra work. The sacrifice of time involved in redoing the assignment may help the child succeed in later life.

We need to instill in our children a mindset to sacrifice for the success that they desire—and to do so all year long. The last week of school, students in danger of failing begin to act nicely to their teachers while making some small attempt to raise their grades to a D in order to pass the course. It is too little, too late. They remind me of the proverbial sluggard:

> Go to the ant, O sluggard, observe her ways and be wise, which, having no chief, officer or ruler, prepares her food in the summer and gathers her provision in the harvest. How long will you lie down, O sluggard? When will you arise from your sleep? "A little sleep, a little slumber, a little folding of the hands to rest"—your poverty will come in like a vagabond and your need like an armed man (Proverbs 6:6-11).

Unfortunately, too many students wait too late to sacrifice. Had they sacrificed all year long—paid attention in class, gone to the library, and studied harder at the beginning of the school term—they would be in a progressive position to succeed.

Bill Cosby purposely enrolled his son in difficult classes under the disciplined instructors at Morehouse College. He knew that if his son would sacrifice and endure the challenging college curriculum, he would be better positioned for success in his career. Students who cannot or will not endure the discipline of their instructors will likely falter when they later enter the work place. Disciplined teachers prepare their students for the work environment, and the wise parent will encourage and model the sacrifice necessary to succeed.

As parents, we must talk to our children about sacrifices. We should make them do the best they can. The question is not whether they made a better grade than everybody else, but did they do the best they could? When they do not, make them do it over. Make them turn off the television and write the paper over! If the teacher asked for a five-page paper and our child wrote four and a half pages, tell him or her to write that additional half page.

My wife and I both made sacrifices for our education. We both worked full time, raised four children, attended school full time, and stayed on the dean's list. Unmarried students who attended college at their parent's expense regularly said to me, "If I were married, I would have more time, and could make better grades." Now, isn't that strange? When I left school at the end of the day, I went to work while they went to the gym. I came home to engage with the children; they went to their dorm room to play cards. I had less time than they had, but I made the decision to sacrifice personal pleasures in order to do the required academic work and spend time with my family.

SACRIFICE LEADS TO SUCCESS IN OUR CAREER.

Remember, he who has the ball shall be tackled. If someone's job is to play football, they cannot complain because someone tackles them. Tackling the running back comes with the territory. It is part of the sacrifice necessary to succeed.

Whether our career is to play football, build houses, or teach schoolchildren, we must be willing to sacrifice in order to succeed at our career. There is no guarantee that we will be promoted in our career, but we can make some necessary sacrifices in case success wants to come our way. That requires a willing attitude to go above and beyond.

Many admire and applaud those who have succeeded in their careers, yet they are unwilling to walk the road of sacrifice that was needed to achieve that success. Those who are unwilling to sacrifice often lay claim and campaign for a redistribution of the wealth obtained by those who do sacrifice. Others complain about how the "system" and unfavorable "others" have hindered their upward mobility. The real culprit is their unwillingness to sacrifice.

Picture a game of basketball. Five players are on the floor playing and five players are on the bench. The game is tight and no substitution can be made. The number six man, who sits on the bench, complains every time a player misses a shot. "I could have made that shot," he grumbles. "The coach should put me in the game. I know I'm better than any of the players out there right now. Why doesn't the coach put me in the game?" He sits, complains, and criticizes—but did he show up early for practice? Did he put in extra hours in order to hone his skills? Did he sacrifice the time and effort necessary in order to become the player he thought he was? Was he willing to make the sacrifices necessary to really be the better player? He was not, yet when the game is over, he shares in the celebration.

Success demands sacrifices. When we sacrifice, we succeed and can celebrate together without guilt. We will succeed only to the extent that we are willing to sacrifice for the success we desire. When we refuse to sacrifice—whether for our family, school, or career—we prove that we are not interested in experiencing success. No matter what we say, if we are unwilling to sacrifice, we have proved that we do not really care about success. We may say we do, but our actions speak louder than our words. God wants us to express our willingness to sacrifice—regularly and verbally. We should get in the habit of saying how we will sacrifice.

We will close this chapter on the relationship of success and sacrifice with three cautions.

1. We must not sacrifice beyond our personal integrity. God informed believers that it would be of no value to them to sacrifice their bodies to be burned when they did not love (see 1 Corinthians 13:3). Similarly, if our sacrifice causes other to fail, our sacrifice is no longer warranted. Parents, for example, should not do without so that their children can have more to waste. It is unwise to subsidize negligence. Similarly, if our sacrifice causes others to fail, our sacrifice is no longer warranted.

2. We must not sacrifice when people use our sacrifice for what is unrighteous. Parents should not give up their freedom in order to baby-sit grandchildren while their parents attend another drug party.

3. We must stop sacrificing for people when they no longer appreciate it. Parents should provide for their children, but if their children are disrespectful, negligent, and lazy, the parents need to make changes, including reevaluating their support.

THOUGHT PROVOKERS

1. Has anything happened to plague the success of the Black family? If so what and why? How has it affected the Black family? What should be done? What will you do to reverse the trend?

2. How has sacrifice led to success within your family? Give specific instances of sacrifices and the resulting success.

3. How has sacrifice led to success within your career, or in any other area of your life? Give specific instances of sacrifices and the resulting success. Was the sacrifice worth it?

Chapter 5

FUNDAMENTALS OF SACRIFICE

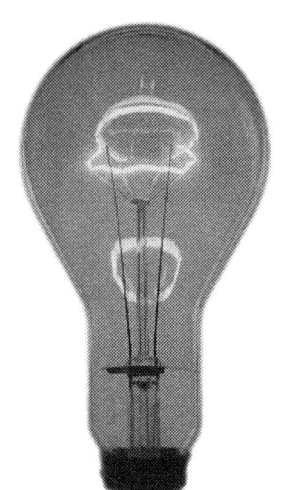

I n this chapter, we will learn about three fundamentals of sacrifice, the proper use of which will bring about success. Fundamentals have to do with foundations. They are the elementary laws that govern the proper fitting and fabrication of an organism or organization. Fundamentals add clarity and cohesion to the design.

THE PRINCIPLE OF SACRIFICE

Sacrifice is a deliberate, calculated decision to go above and beyond, as in this description of the early (and very successful) church:

> Everyone kept feeling a sense of awe; and many wonders and signs were taking place through the apostles. And all those who had believed were together and had all things in common; and they began selling their property and possessions and

were sharing them with all, as anyone might have need (Acts 2:43-45).

These believers deliberately decided to sacrifice—to go above and beyond in order to help. Thousands of Jews had traveled to Jerusalem to celebrate the Passover and had remained to celebrate the feast of Pentecost, which was fifty days after the Passover. The word *Pentecost* literally refers to fifty. Those Jews had economically prepared themselves for a fifty-day excursion. They had no idea that the gospel would be preached and they would linger days longer in Jerusalem. Those who were in need were not needy because of negligence. They were in need because they had stayed longer to become further instructed in the gospel, which enabled them to be more effective with their own evangelism when they returned home. Rather than this being a case of benevolence, it really was a financial support for evangelism—the one mission of the church. Time and time again, believers sacrificed; they deliberately decided to go above and beyond.

> And the congregation of those who believed were of one heart and soul; and not one of them claimed that anything belonging to him was his own, but all things were common property to them. And with great power the apostles were giving testimony to the resurrection of the Lord Jesus, and abundant grace was upon them all. For there was not a needy person among them,

for all who were owners of land or houses would sell them and bring the proceeds of the sales and lay them at the apostles' feet, and they would be distributed to each as any had need (Acts 4:32-35).

THE PURPOSE OF SACRIFICE

At times sacrifice is a determined calculation, but at other times it is a divine commission, as in this account from Jesus' life. "Looking at him, Jesus felt a love for him and said to him, 'One thing you lack: go and sell all you possess and give to the poor, and you will have treasure in heaven; and come, follow Me' " (Mark 10:21). The Lord decided how much the rich ruler's sacrifice should be.

Time and time again, God specifically requests His sacrifice, and He does so for a purpose. Sacrifice enables covenant people to do business with God according to His guidelines. It allows God to bless His covenant people with His covenant promises. God made a covenant with Abraham in Genesis chapter 12. He promised to bless Abraham and be favorable to those who were favorable to him. He promised to curse those who refused to be favorable to Abraham. In order to receive the covenant promises, Abraham had to sacrifice his own preferences and walk in God's path.

Peter asked what they were going to get for making sacrifice, that is, for leaving everything in order to follow Jesus. The Lord promised bountiful blessings to His disciples who made such sacrifice:

> Jesus said, "Truly I say to you, there is no one who has left house or brothers or sisters or mother or father or children or farms, for My sake and for the gospel's sake, but that he will receive a hundred times as much now in the present age, houses and brothers and sisters and mothers and children and farms, along with persecutions; and in the age to come, eternal life" (Mark 10:29-30).

Only by sacrifice could they multiply in this manner. If the rich ruler had not left church early, he would have discovered that Jesus was not trying to take something from him, but was trying to give something to him.

Sacrifice enables covenant people to posses covenant promises, but sacrifice also encourages those who are not covenant people to position themselves to posses covenant promises. When unbelievers saw how God's people prospered, they too wanted to make sacrifice. Success attracts. After believers sacrificed, unbelievers were attracted daily to become believers (see Acts 2:43-47). Over and over again, the sacrifice by believers persuaded unbelievers to believe: "And all the more believers in the Lord, multitudes of men and women, were constantly added to their number" (Acts 5:14). Sacrifice enables covenant people to posses covenant promises, but it also enlists non-covenant people to position themselves to receive the covenant promises. There is a purpose for sacrifice and a principle of sacrifice.

Sacrifice is painful to the immature and the unspiritual. We give but grudgingly. We see sacrifice as a burden depleting our resources. God is not trying to break our bank account. He is not interested in seeing us become broke. He is not trying to take all our money, time, and talents. That seems to be the misunderstanding of the rich ruler (see Mark 10:17-22). No doubt he said to himself, "I worked hard and accumulated these possessions, and now this fellow has come along and wants me to just give it away and be broke. I don't have time for Him nor a church like that." Yet he had just called Jesus a good teacher (see verse 17). Obviously, he looked for a statement of compliment and was shocked when he received a statement of complement.

For the immature and unspiritual, sacrifice is like medicine to children. They see it as a burden to their taste rather than a blessing to their health. The mature and spiritual, on the other hand, willingly make sacrifices with pleasure and joy. They understand that sacrifice is not a burden but a blessing. They understand that God is not trying to deplete their resources but rather He is trying to replenish their resources. Imagine how the rich ruler would have felt if he ever discovered that he could have been 100 times richer. A hundred-fold blessing is a good business transaction in anyone's book.

Sacrifice contradicts fleshly feelings. The very idea of sacrifice is contrary to our fleshly feelings. The more we are controlled by our fleshly feelings, the more difficulty we will experience making sacrifice. Human nature says, "Always keep all your stuff. Buy larger storage bins so that you can keep everything you accumulate. Remember: He who dies with the most toys wins."

God's response to this fleshly attitude is the same response He gave to the rich man who tried to horde his fortune: "But God said to him, 'You fool! This very night your soul is required of you; and now who will own what you have prepared?' So is the man who stores up treasure for himself, and is not rich toward God" (Luke 12:20-21).

The very nature of sacrifice requires that it be made when we do not feel like it. Sacrifice is inconsistent with the flesh, but is consistent with faith. Believers walk by faith and not by sight (or feelings). Sacrifice must be based upon faith not feelings.

THE PRACTICE OF SACRIFICE

Notice that Jesus did not rebuke the rich man for being rich or for having a good harvest of crops; He rebuked him because he had put his trust and faith in them instead of in the Lord, and was not generous with them. God does not want us to be poor, but He does want us to have a godly attitude toward what He gives us. That means being generous with the blessings He has blessed us with, as we saw in the example of the early church in the book of Acts, and it also means taking care of the blessings He gives us. Often that involves sacrifice. If He blesses us with a nice house or a good business, we will have to sacrifice to maintain them. Things of value are obtained by sacrifice and maintained by sacrifice. Sacrifices in one generation require compatible sacrifices in the next in order to maintain the success achieved. The moment we stop sacrificing to maintain something, it will begin to deteriorate. The sacrifices needed to develop a thriving business are the same sacrifices needed to maintain that thriving business. This is even true of relationships—family, friends, church, and business.

A refusal to sacrifice may cause God to take away what He has given. In Matthew chapter 25, to one man, the master gave five talents; to another, two talents, and to another, one talent. The men who received five and two talents sacrificed to maintain what they had been given—and they received more. The man who had one talent made no sacrifices. He not only did not accumulate more, but he lost the one talent that he had received.

What will you sacrifice?

THOUGHT PROVOKERS

1. In the past, have you seen sacrifice as a burden or blessing?

2. As a result of reading this chapter, has your concept of sacrifice changed? How?

3. Where is God calling you to sacrifice? What success might be the result?

Chapter 6

PERSECUTION GROWS IN THE SOIL OF SUCCESS

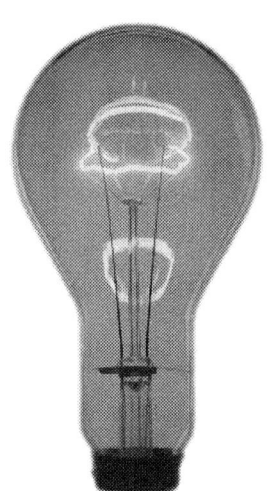

Peter began to say to Him, "Behold, we have left everything and followed You." Jesus said, "Truly I say to you, there is no one who has left house or brothers or sisters or mother or father or children or farms, for My sake and for the gospel's sake, but that he will receive a hundred times as much now in the present age, houses and brothers and sisters and mothers and children and farms, along with persecutions; and in the age to come, eternal life" (Mark 10:28-30).

Digging in the garden of sacrificial success, Jesus uncovered the thorn of persecution. Peter announced the valley of their sacrifice, but Jesus announced the mountain of their success. His statement—that along with the rewards for following Jesus comes persecution—is astounding and seems out of character with our concept or definition of success, but it is part of the package. The word persecution literally means "to put to flight." It means to irritate a person until that person runs away. The persecutor then follows after the persecuted in order to provide more irritation.

Persecution is Satan's purpose-driven affliction. Satan intends to irritate us until he drives us away from the ultimate purpose of God. Satan knows that God has a purpose for every individual. Satan believes that the adequate affliction will drive us away from the purpose of God. God recommended the faith of Job, but Satan believed that God supernaturally protected Job. He argued that if God allowed him to irritate Job, he would drive Job away from the purpose of God (see Job 1:8-12). Satan has not changed his beliefs nor his tactics. In fact, he believes the same about us—you and me. Yes, Satan believes that through irritation he can drive us away from the purpose of God. Therefore, just as success comes, persecution is also sure to come. Success waters the ground in which persecution grows.

But we ask, "Where am I likely to find persecution?" Let's consider the soils where we are most likely to find persecution growing.

PHYSIOLOGICAL AFFLICTION

We are likely to find persecution growing in the soil of physical discomfort. Therefore, Satan provides physical affliction that will discomfort us, intending ultimately to lead us away from the purpose of God.

How many times have we heard someone say, "I was having a bad day, so I just lost my temper and said something I should not have said"? How does a headache affect the mouth? More to the point, how does a headache affect the heart, for "the things that proceed out of the mouth come from the heart, and those defile the man" (Matthew 15:18). This encounter is a trick of the devil. Through the physical discomfort of a headache, Satan has driven us away from the purpose of God to be slow to speak (see James 1:19). Physical affliction has led us away from God's purpose for our life.

After the apostle Paul's conversion, he spoke about his life prior to his conversion:

> I am a Jew, born in Tarsus of Cilicia, but brought up in this city, educated under Gamaliel, strictly according to the law of our fathers, being zealous for God just as you all are today. I persecuted this Way to the death, binding and putting both men and women into prisons, as also the high priest and all the Council of the elders can testify. From

them I also received letters to the brethren, and started off for Damascus in order to bring even those who were there to Jerusalem as prisoners to be punished (Acts 22:3-5).

He caused physical discomfort, putting both men and women in prison and even persecuting them to death. Let us ask him several questions.

"Saul, what are you going to do?"

"I am going to persecute them."

"How are you going to persecute them?"

"I'm going to cause physical discomfort."

Satan worked through Saul to make believers physically uncomfortable. Through the persecution of physical discomfort, Satan intended to drive them away from the purpose of God. Satan is well aware that many are unwilling to endure physical discomfort. On any given Sunday that it rains, church attendance falls.

PSYCHOLOGICAL AFFLICTION

We are also likely to find persecution growing in the soil of mental affliction. Mental affliction brings about discouragement, and the devil definitely wants to discourage us. He knows he can get us away from the purpose of God if he discomforts us, but he also knows that he can lead us away from the purpose of God if he discourages us. In either category, he severs us from the purpose of God.

The disciples asked Jesus if blindness was due to personal sin or parental sin (see John 9:2). Jesus informed them that neither the sin of the man nor his parents caused his blindness. After answering their question, Jesus spat on the ground, anointed the man's eyes, and gave him sight. A major controversy erupted about who was responsible for giving this man his eyesight. Can you imagine that? A man who had been blind all his life could now see, and people had the audacity to ask who did it. It was a miracle beyond miracles, and the most important issue to them was, "Who did it?"

Some charged the man with impersonating the blind man. They asked his parents for verification that this was their son who had been born blind. After receiving affirmation, they asked his parents how their son had received his sight. Because they were afraid of the Jews, his parents denied all knowledge of who had healed their son, and sent the interrogators to their son. They were afraid because the Jews had already agreed to excommunicate from the synagogue anyone who confessed Christ. His parents did not want to endure this mental discouragement. That fear of persecution proved too discouraging for them. Confessing truth would isolate them from their friends.

Persecution grows in the ground of both physical discomfort and mental discouragement.

We must know the purpose of persecution and work to minimize our persecution. We must resolve not to abandon the purpose of God in spite of physical discomfort. We must willingly sacrifice, going above and beyond, and enduring physical discomfort. Why? To accomplish the purpose of God. We must press through physical discomforts and mental discouragement to accomplish the purpose of God. Sacrificial success waters the ground in which persecution grows.

Satan is the source of persecution. He wants to sever us from the purpose of God. Regardless of what happens, we should not let the devil drive us away from the purpose of God. When we are persecuted, we are under a satanic attack.

Persecution is inherently attached to sacrificial success. In the verses from Mark that we quoted at the beginning of this chapter, Jesus intentionally not incidentally placed persecution in the same context. People who make the greatest sacrifices are often the ones who receive the most persecution. Often it seems the more that parents sacrifice for their children, the less their children appreciate it. Church leaders invest themselves helping members, only to be resented by those whom they have helped. When we decide to sacrifice, we must remember that we may be persecuted for doing so. Persecution comes with the territory.

As we learned earlier, he who has the ball shall be tackled. Persecution is a part of the game of life, just like it is part of the game of football. If we understand Mark 10:30, when persecution happens to us, we will not be alarmed nor stop to cry. Paul writes to Timothy, "Indeed, all who desire to live godly in Christ Jesus will be persecuted" (2 Timothy 3:12). It is going to happen. Sacrificial success waters the ground in which persecution grows. God promised to multiply their success, but reminded them that persecution tagged along.

Believers in other countries may know this more intimately than those of us in the United States. In countries such as Sudan, Nigeria, Ethiopia, China, India, Indonesia, North Korea, Cuba, Vietnam, and elsewhere, Christians are regularly persecuted for their faith. They have had to learn how to live with persecution. Every day, believers in these countries are harassed, arrested, imprisoned, tortured, and even killed for following Jesus. Are they sacrificing? Absolutely. Are they successful? Yes, although their success is not in the world's eyes, and may not even be in this life. Yet the principle of sacrifice leading to success is still valid, because in some instances the church is growing faster than in countries where believers are free to worship.

Persecuted believers in China, for example, say, "Don't pray for our persecution to stop, because that is causing the church to grow; instead pray that we will be strong in the midst of the persecution." God will give us the grace to endure persecution. It is ours for the taking, although many choose not to take it.

How can we endure persecution? What we think about what happens to us is most important. What we think determines how we feel, and how we feel will dictate how we respond. We must get control of our response. Those who think and feel inappropriately will always behave inappropriately. The war starts not in the behaving phase but in the thinking phase.

GOD GIVES GRACE TO AVOID RETALIATION.

Retaliation will cause confusion and cause us to lose the battle of persecution. Those who retaliate are likely to lose the war on persecution. Consequently, we must be careful. God gives us the grace that is necessary so that we can endure persecution without retaliation. Jesus did not retaliate against His persecutors. He refrained from both verbal and physical retaliation toward his persecutors.

> For what credit is there if, when you sin and are harshly treated, you endure it with patience? But, if when you do what is right and suffer for it you patiently endure it, this finds favor with God. For you have been called for this purpose, since Christ also suffered for you, leaving you an example for you to follow in His steps, who committed no sin, nor was any deceit found in

His mouth; and while being reviled, He did not revile in return; while suffering, He uttered no threats, but kept entrusting Himself to Him who judges righteously; and He Himself bore our sins in His body on the cross, so that we might die to sin and live to righteousness; for by His wounds you were healed (1 Peter 2:20-24).

Jesus suffered patiently as an example for us. When we follow His example, we find favor in the eyes of God. Because of His willingness to refrain from retaliation, He became so successful. "He learned obedience from the things which He suffered. And having been made perfect, He became to all those who obey Him the source of eternal salvation" (Hebrews 5:8-9). Favor (success) in the eyes of God validates our suffering. We can and should not retaliate.

As parents, we must teach our children to refrain from retaliation. What do we tell our sons to do when another little boy hits him? Do we tell them one thing, but demonstrate another? Do they observe us seeking retaliation against those who have hurt us? Are we motivated by the drive to get even? If we are, then our children will be, too. Getting even can be a tricky business. When do we really get even? The best way—the only way, in fact—to truly get even with our enemies is to bring them up to God's level not by taking ourselves down to the devil's level. Those with a spiritual conscience feel worse, like losers, after retaliation.

GOD GIVES GRACE TO ENDURE REJECTION.

The devil uses rejection to distract good people. Some are held hostage by the spirit of retaliation, while others surrender to the spirit of rejection. Often, rejection and retaliation work together simultaneously.

Rejection makes peer pressure powerful. Peer pressure says, "If you refuse to conform, we will isolate you. If you conform, we will include you." The need to fit in can overwhelm many people, who surrender to their need to be included. Rejection is a powerful force, but the fear of rejection persuades only those who possess an inordinate need to feel accepted.

Do we feel rejected if a close friend forgets to include us in his social plans? Do we have the same feeling if that same friend refuses to include us in his work plans? Normally, we do not experience rejection as strongly in work situations as we do in social situations. We can feel rejected when we are excluded from the fellowship meal, but not if we are excluded form the clean-up detail. Therefore, rejection exerts its greatest power in matters where there is a group to which we are not invited to be a part.

Rejection affects only those who have a need to be accepted by those who are rejecting them in the first place. So unless we feel a need to be accepted by a person or a group of people, then their rejection has no power over us at all.

The important thing to remember is that God has accepted us. Time and time again in the book of Ephesians, He reminds His people that He has accepted them on the basis of their perfect savior, Jesus, not on the basis of their perfect performance. Being in Christ—in His body—we are included in Kingdom fellowship.

Evidently, the parents of the formerly blind man of John chapter 9 wanted to be included in the synagogue events. Therefore, the threat of excommunication persecuted them to the point of denying how their son had received his sight. They denied because they feared the Jews. They did not want to be the only couple in the community banned from church. The feeling of rejection became more important than the celebration of their child receiving his eyesight. Feelings of rejection will cause confusion and unhappiness in our lives.

Eagles do not flock. They fly alone. Buzzards, on the other hand, will flock. Eagles do not flock and buzzards do not soar like eagles. We must learn how to walk alone with God and be fully content with Him. We must learn to enjoy our time alone with God. We do not have to feel bad because no one called us this week. We do not have to feel rejected when we no longer seem to be the center of social acceptance.

Luke recorded the events of Jesus' last trip through Samaria as He traveled toward Jerusalem (see Luke 9:51-56). The local Samaritans refused to welcome Jesus because He was going to

Jerusalem, so His apostles, James and John, felt rejected and asked for permission to retaliate by providing a portable hell to consume the citizens: "Lord, do You want us to command fire down from heaven and consume them?" (verse 54).

Jesus rebuked them and denied their request. They were unaware of their own spirit, but He reminded them of His ultimate purpose of God. He came to save lives not destroy lives. He helped them to win over that instance of persecution. Had Jesus not intervened, His disciples would have sinned and wandered away from the purpose of God. Jesus refused to allow persecution to hinder His fulfillment of the purpose of God. Had He fallen for the persecution trap, He would have missed the success that came with sacrifice.

A mark of maturity is the willingness to rebuke those who are behaving in an ungodly manner, even if it is on our behalf. Jesus could have said, "Since I did not tell them to do it, I am innocent of their bad behavior." That seems to be the attitude of the notorious convicted murderer Charles Manson. When asked in a television interview if he ordered the murder of Sharon Tate, he said, "I never told nobody to kill anybody; they just knew what to do." I do not know whether he did or did not order her murder, but his argument evaded the question of whether he was responsible for the murder.

We should never abandon the purpose of God just to retaliate. Retaliation is always the wrong choice. We should not abandon the purpose of God in an effort to obtain sinful gratification.

Nor should we ever abandon the purpose of God just to satisfy our feeling of rejection. Remember, our sole objective in life is to please God. When we please Him, He will flood our lives with all things that are necessary to endure persecution. His grace is always available to us.

THOUGHT PROVOKERS

1. Where have you suffered persecution on the road to success? What was your response? Are you satisfied with that response? Is God?

2. Is the Holy Spirit speaking to you about an area where you have sought retaliation against someone who has hurt you? What should your response be?

3. How has rejection affected the decisions you have made?

Chapter 7

SUCCESSFULLY RESISTING PEER PRESSURE

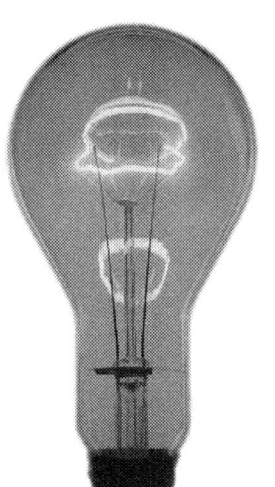

We have learned that success is not just a good idea, but it is a God idea. God desires for us to be successful in every area of our lives, and He gives us the tools and grace to do so; He leaves the choice to us whether we will take them or leave them. In the next few chapters, we will examine specific areas where God desires to give us success, and study the tools He provides for us to achieve that success.

We will begin with the area of peer pressure; there is positive peer pressure and negative peer pressure, and if we are to be successful, we need to learn how to successfully resist the negative type. Many people believe that peer pressure is something that affects only young children or teenagers, but adults are extremely susceptible to it, also. Our peers are those whom we seek favor from. Psychologists call them our "significant others." Our peers are those with whom we want to be significant. We call the influence from our significant others "peer pressure." Peer pressure affects the young as well as the aged. It affects saints as well as sinners. Not one of us is immune to peer pressure.

Peer pressure can be destructive or constructive. A prime example of destructive peer pressure in the Bible is the story of Pilate. John chapter 19 reports that Pilate examined Jesus and discovered that He was innocent, and time and time again, he reported his findings to the people. In spite of Jesus' innocence, however, Pilate delivered Him to be crucified. Isn't that amazing? The evidence for innocence was staring Pilate in the face, yet he delivered Jesus to be crucified. It was as astounding as if in a modern-day courtroom the jurors announced their verdict of "innocent," yet the judge asked the prosecuting attorney, "What do you want me to do with him?" That is exactly what Pilate did. He determined Jesus was innocent, yet asked the prosecutors for their preference—and then honored their wishes. Why? Pilate succumbed to the destructive pressure from his peers.

Another example of destructive peer pressure is in Acts 5:1-10, which tells the sad story of how Sapphira allowed her husband, Ananias, to persuade her to lie to the Holy Spirit. For participating in this conspiracy, they both died.

Not all peer pressure is destructive; it can also be constructive, as in this example from the book of Hebrews: "Let us consider how to stimulate one another to love and good deeds, not forsaking our own assembling together, as is the habit of some, but encouraging one another; and all the more as you see the day drawing near" (Hebrews 10:24-25). The author is telling believers they need to encourage each other—a good form of peer pressure.

In this chapter, we will look at destructive peer pressure and learn how we can successfully resist it. Regardless of which peers exert the pressure, we can successfully resist. We must resist. We are individually accountable to God for our behavior. The question is, how can we successfully resist destructive peer pressure? How could Pilate have successfully resisted? The answer to the latter question will also answer the former question.

INVESTIGATE THE NICKELS.

One of the ways that our peers can seek to influence us is with money or financial favors. They approach us with situations that appear to be financially advantageous. Too often we go along with the program.

When Pilate feebly attempted to release Jesus, the Jews questioned his allegiance to Caesar. "If you release this Man, you are no friend of Caesar; everyone who makes himself out to be a king opposes Caesar" (John 19:12). As king, Caesar controlled Pilate's purse strings. He had the power to reduce his financial livelihood and even to remove him from office.

Earlier the Jews had charged Jesus with opposing the paying of taxes to Caesar (see Luke 23:1). If Pilate sided with one who opposed paying taxes to Caesar, how could Caesar possibly remain supportive of Pilate? The mere reminder of Caesar overwhelmed Pilate's better judgment. "When Pilate heard these words, he brought Jesus out, and sat down on the judgment seat…And he said to the Jews, 'Behold, your King!'" (John 19:13-14).

Imagine how upset our government would be if no tax money came in. Imagine what would happen to political officials if the tax money evaporated overnight. In the midst of an election year, half the candidates would quit running if the government became bankrupt.

When Pilate heard that charge, the money overruled his better judgment. In spite of the fact that he knew that Jesus was innocent, the "nickels" caused him to overrule his better judgment and he delivered Jesus to be crucified.

Beware of unethical and unfair gain. Usually such gain is short-lived and shallowly enjoyed. People who live by crookedness and treachery rarely enjoy lasting joy. Therefore, we must always investigate the nickels. There is nothing wrong with pursuing legitimate business ventures. However, very few if any people exist to give away money. Few if any have a proven wealth-making process that they are willing to share. Yet, frequently people claim to have a "new" wealth scheme that all the brilliant minds have heretofore overlooked. They promise us that our economic status will quickly flourish. Many swiftly follow these lures.

The old adage to "look before you leap" still is true. Pilate should have asked questions—the same questions that we should ask: Is my integrity for sale? Can I earn an adequate income doing business with integrity? Will I be able to survive if I don't sell my integrity? Will I be able to live with myself if I do? If I follow this trend, where will it lead? Where will I be next year?

Many have followed financial get-rich-quick schemes and wandered further and further from the truth and the church. God warned those who were already rich, "Instruct those who are rich in this present world not to be conceited or to fix their hope on the uncertainty of riches, but on God, who richly supplies us with all things to enjoy" (1 Timothy 6:17). He also warned those who wanted to be rich:

> But those who want to get rich fall into temptation and a snare and many foolish and harmful desires which plunge men into ruin and destruction. For the love of money is a root of all sorts of evil, and some by longing for it have wandered away from the faith and pierced themselves with many griefs (1 Timothy 6:9-10).

How can we successfully resist peer pressure? One way is to thoroughly investigate the nickels.

IGNORE THE NOISE.

Our peers use noise—volume of voice without clarity of substance—to influence us. The Jews used noise to influence Pilate to release Jesus to be crucified. They never answered Pilate's questions, "Why? What evil has He done?" They just increased their volume of voice calling for His crucifixion.

> But the governor said to them, "Which of the two do you want me to release for you?" And they said, "Barabbas." Pilate said to them, "Then what shall I do with Jesus who is called Christ?" They all said, "Crucify Him!" And he said, "Why, what evil has He done?" But they kept shouting all the more, saying, "Crucify Him!" When Pilate saw that he was accomplishing nothing, but rather that a riot was starting, he took water and washed his hands in front of the crowd, saying, "I am innocent of this Man's blood; see to that yourselves." And all the people said, "His blood shall be on us and on our children!" Then he released Barabbas for them; but after having Jesus scourged, he handed Him over to be crucified (Matthew 27:21-26).

Offering them a choice between Barabbas and Jesus, Pilate asked the crowd for their opinion. When they chose Barabbas, he asked, "Then what shall I do with Jesus who is called Christ?" No judicial basis existed upon which to charge Jesus, yet they attempted to charge Him. When Pilate asked, "Why, what evil has He done?" they had no legitimate answer. Yet, they expressed their desire to crucify Him. Saying the same thing over and over again, they just made more noise. Their passion raced toward a riotous frenzy as they kept shouting, but they never answered Pilate's question.

When Pilate realized that a riot, a civil disturbance, was about to erupt right in his presence, he tried to distance himself from the whole ungodly affair by declaring his innocence. After this declaration, Pilate released Barabbas. Who is this Barabbas? He was a prisoner who had participated in an insurrection or riot and committed murder during it (see Mark 15:7). Yes, Barabbas was a murderous rioter. Noise will lead us to release a murderous rioter in an attempt to prevent a riot. Noise is destructive peer pressure that destroys our better judgment. The best way to deal with this type of peer pressure is to ignore the noise.

INTERPRET THE NUMBERS.

Not only must we investigate nickels and ignore noise, but we must also interpret the numbers. Our peers influence us with numbers. They will say to us, "But everybody is doing this.

There are some significant people who have agreed with me, and if you don't go along with us, you are going to be opposing your significant people."

In the entire episode of Pilate condemning Jesus, only one person, a woman, spoke up on behalf of Jesus. "While he [Pilate] was sitting on the judgment seat, his wife sent him a message, saying, 'Have nothing to do with that righteous Man; for last night I suffered greatly in a dream because of Him'" (Matthew 27:19). Not even the twelve who were close to him, not even His inner circle—Peter, James and John—spoke up to defend Him. Only Pilate's wife spoke up on behalf of Jesus. Pilate allowed the numbers to destroy his better judgment; therefore he surrendered to the peer pressure of the Jews.

When we are faced with numbers trying to influence us, we can successfully resist the peer pressure by asking ourselves questions. First, we seek to discover *what* is right, and then we look to see *who* is right.

1. What are these people really saying? If Pilate had asked that question, he would have discovered that they were saying the same thing they said before: "Crucify Him! Crucify Him!"

2. Are they arguing wisely or foolishly? It is foolish to crucify an innocent man, and Pilate knew this, but the numbers persuaded him to act otherwise.

3. Would rational reasoning lead to their same conclusion, or would it lead to another conclusion? Are these people reaching an intelligent conclusion?

4. Who are these people that are trying to influence me? Do they have my best interests at heart, or are they looking only to their own personal, selfish interests? Are these people themselves failures?

Those who kept saying, "Crucify Him" were failures. They had lost numerous encounters with Jesus. They had been embarrassed by Jesus. Every time they brought Him a question, He gave them an answer that baffled their minds. They were failures. For years, they had tried to trap Jesus. They had a personal vendetta against Him.

Pilate had the power to release Jesus. He had the will to release Jesus, for he made efforts to release Him (see John 19:7-12), but for some reason he simply could never get it together; he never had the willpower. Destructive peer pressure prevented him from getting it together. Destructive peer pressure will keep us from getting it together, too.

We must be determined not to surrender to the destructive influence of peer pressure. God has given us the tools to resist—investigate the nickels, ignore the noise, and interpret the numbers—and He will give us the grace we need to be successful.

THOUGHT PROVOKERS

1. How can we determine when peer pressure is destructive and when it is constructive? Should peers pressure peers? If so, how much pressure should peers exert upon other peers?

2. Who or what group shares the most nickels, makes the most noise, and has the majority of the numbers within our society?

3. Think about this statement: "Some people follow the style while others set the style." Is it all right to be different?

Chapter 8

SUCCESSFULLY RESISTING OPPOSITION

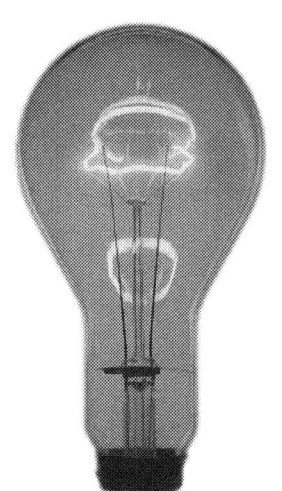

Life is not always easy, nor is life always "fair." Life is not always a downhill coast. As a matter of fact, life is not always played on a level plain. Frequently, obstacles lodge themselves in our pathway and cause life to become an uphill struggle played out against powerful opposition. That is simply the way it is. Therefore, we must learn to engage opposition successfully. Engaging opposition often provides momentum that leads to success. For every action, there is an equal and opposite reaction. The strength of the opposing action increases the strength of the resisting reaction, elevating our potential power.

Take the case of Katherine, who worked in a small-town factory. Katherine's immediate supervisor criticized her and her work every day. She sensed that he did not want her to work in his department nor even for the company, but she needed her job and was determined to do well enough to remain employed.

Daily her supervisor agitated her about her job performance. Daily she determined to become more skilled at her work. Eventually, her prowess became evident and even her contentious supervisor could no longer deny the quality and quantity of her work. Reluctantly he began to admire and compliment her work, and they became tolerably peaceful toward each other. A few years later, the factory began to reduce its operation and lay off employees. Eventually the owners decided to shut down the entire facility, but they needed a skeletal crew of the most skilled employees to work an additional six months after all other employees had been terminated. Because of Katherine's proficiency, her supervisor recommended that she be among the employees who stayed the additional six months, and the owners agreed.

Why did Katherine succeed at remaining employed an additional six months? Because she was one of the most proficienct employees. How and why did she become so proficient? She became proficient in response to the opposition of her supervisor. Opposition drove her to be a better worker. Opposition resulted in success.

We do not like to endure rude or harsh supervisors, teachers, family members, or others. No one does. However, that very opposition could catapult us to greater heights of success. When the apostles received mistreatment at the hands of unfair men, they rejoiced that they were counted worthy to suffer shame for the name of the Lord (see Acts 5:41). In times of opposition, we, too, should thank God—not for the pain of the discipline, but for the progress that it provides.

In 605 BC during the reign of Jehoiakim, king of Judah, the Babylonian King Nebuchadnezzar attacked Jerusalem and deported many Jews, including Daniel, to Babylon (see 2 Chronicles 36:5-9 and 2 Kings 24:1-5). Nebuchadnezzar deported even more Jews to Babylon in 597 BC during the reign of Jehoiachin, king of Judah, including Ezekiel (see 2 Chronicles 36:10 and 2 Kings 24:6-16). Eleven years later, during the reign of Zedekiah, king of Judah, Nebuchadnezzar attacked Jerusalem, totally destroying the temple and the walls of the city (see 2 Chronicles 36:11-21 and 2 Kings 24:17—25:30).

It was nearly a half century later—538 BC—before some of the Jews returned to Jerusalem with Zerubbabel and rebuilt the temple in Jerusalem (see Ezra 3:8). Eighty years later, in 458 BC, more Jews along with the prophet Ezra returned to Jerusalem (see Ezra chapters 7-8). Nehemiah returned twelve years after that and rebuilt the walls around Jerusalem (see Nehemiah chapters 1-3). We will pick up the story there, because Nehemiah is an excellent example of how to successfully resist opposition.

Nehemiah had heard about the desolate condition of

Jerusalem, and talked to God about it (see Nehemiah 1:1-11). In response, God gave Nehemiah His vision to rebuild the walls around the city of Jerusalem (Nehemiah 2:11-12)—but Nehemiah did not complete the task without encountering much opposition. Interestingly, the name *Nehemiah* means "Comfort of Jehovah." Indeed, Nehemiah needed much comfort from the Lord because the opposition that he and the people faced threatened to demoralize them. Nehemiah cried out to the Lord in the face of the taunts that the enemy hurled at them: "Hear, O our God, how we are despised! Return their reproach on their own heads and give them up for plunder in a land of captivity. Do not forgive their iniquity and let not their sin be blotted out before You, for they have demoralized the builders" (Nehemiah 4:4-5).

The builders sought to do well—to succeed at the task before them—but the enemy opposed them. Yet the builders maintained their focus in the midst of opposition: "So we built the wall and the whole wall was joined together to half its height, for the people had a mind to work" (Nehemiah 4:6). How did they do it? What can we learn from Nehemiah and the builders that will help us successfully resist opposition that we encounter?

RESIST RIDICULE.

When Sanballat and Tobiah saw Nehemiah and the other Jews rebuilding the wall, their response was to verbally ridicule them:

> Now it came about that when Sanballat heard that we were rebuilding the wall, he became furious and very angry and mocked the Jews. He spoke in the presence of his brothers and the wealthy men of Samaria and said, "What are these feeble Jews doing? Are they going to restore it for themselves? Can they offer sacrifices? Can they finish in a day? Can they revive the stones from the dusty rubble even the burned ones?" Now Tobiah the Ammonite was near him and he said, "Even what they are building—if a fox should jump on it, he would break their stone wall down!" (Nehemiah 4:1-3).

We can only imagine the mocking and laughter that accompanied the ridicule. The response of Nehemiah and the other Jews is significant; they responded to the ridicule with prayer (see verses 4-5) and with continued mental and physical focus (see verse 6). We cannot successfully resist opposition without prayer; with prayer, God will give us the strength to focus mentally and physically on the task before us.

RESIST RUMOR.

When opposition by ridicule did not work, Nehemiah's enemies used another form of opposition: rumor.

> Now when Sanballat, Tobiah, the Arabs, the Ammonites and the Ashdodites heard that the repair of the walls of Jerusalem went on, and that the breaches began to be closed, they were very angry. All of them conspired together to come and fight against Jerusalem and to cause a disturbance in it. But we prayed to our God, and because of them we set up a guard against them day and night (verses 7-9).

Half the work was completed, and Tobiah was getting worried, so he pulled out the weapon of rumor by stirring up trouble against the Jews and threatening the workers with violence. Again, the Jews responded with prayer and with mental and physical focus: "But we prayed to our God, and because of them we set up a guard against them day and night" (verse 9).

Consider the source of the ridicule and rumor. Often people who resort to such means are angry, and Sanballat and Tobiah were no exception. Sanballat was a Moabite and Tobiah was an Ammonite. Years earlier God had excluded the Moabites and Ammonites from His assembly (see Nehemiah 13:1-3, Genesis 19:31-37, and Deuteronomy 23:2-4). Could these men have been jealous?

Nehemiah actually started resisting opposition before it even began. Prior to rebuilding one inch of the wall, he secretly analyzed the situation before him—by conducting a secret, nighttime inspection of the walls of Jerusalem (see Nehemiah 2:13-15). Why did he inspect? Because he wanted to see the human perspective of the situation. Why secretly? Because he was the one with the vision, and initially he was the only one who needed to know the results of his inspection. Working in secret delays opposition and eliminates the need for explanation before the vision has been further revealed.

REINFORCE THE TROOPS.

God gives His vision to an individual but He never intends for the individual to do the work alone. As the leader of the builders and the one with the initial vision to rebuild the wall, Nehemiah not only dealt with the people handing out the opposition, but he also made sure that opposition was not wearing down the people under him. How did he inspire the builders?

First, he helped them to see the *awfulness of their present situation:* "I said to them, 'You see the bad situation we are in, that Jerusalem is desolate and its gates burned by fire'" (Nehemiah 2:17a). The walls protected the city from foreign invasions, and without them, they were defenseless.

Then, he helped them to see the *awesomeness of the future*: "'Come, let us rebuild the wall of Jerusalem so that we will no longer be a reproach.' I told them how the hand of my God had been favorable to me and also about the king's words which he had spoken to me" (Nehemiah 2:17b-18a). With walls, they were fortified and their dignity in the eyes of their neighbors returned.

In the end, we must ask ourselves if what we are facing is opposition, or is it an opportunity disguised as opposition? Our response may very well define the experience. If we surrender and fail, it was opposition. If we resist and succeed, it was an opportunity.

THOUGHT PROVOKERS

1. How would you have responded had you been Katherine? When have you faced opposition in the form of criticism, ridicule, or rumor, and how did you respond? Is there a point when you should surrender to the opposition and call it quits? If so, where is that point?

2. Have you felt God comforting you when you have encountered painful opposition? How does 2 Corinthians 1:3-4 help you?

3. What do you learn about God as you observe the strategies that He provides to help you overcome opposition? Do you pray more often for God to remove your opposition or to make you capable to overcome your opposition?

Chapter 9

SUCCESSFULLY FORGIVING

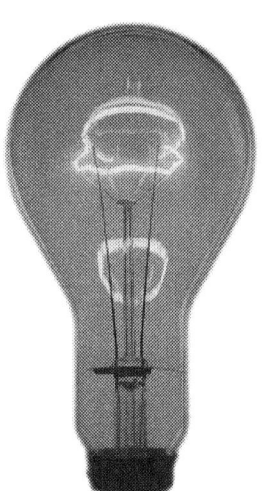

It is virtually impossible to go through life and not be violated, hurt, offended, or betrayed. No one is immune from it. It is part of life. How we respond to those who violate us will be important. Our thoughts and feelings will dictate our response. Therefore, we must intentionally manage our thoughts and feelings. When we mismanage our thoughts and feelings, we allow those who violated us to minimize our success in life. On the other hand, when we think and feel toward our transgressors in a proper and godly manner, we increase the probability of achieving much success.

Joseph, the great-grandson of the patriarch Abraham, endured gross mistreatment from his brothers. And as we will see later in this chapter, he refused to harbor a grudge of resentment. Rather he forgave, and because of his willingness to forgive, he enjoyed great success in Egypt. The annals of history hold his name in high esteem.

Ted Morris, the only son of Frank and Elizabeth Morris

of Pee Dee, Kentucky, was killed by a drunk driver named Tommy Pigage. Ted's death traumatized his entire family, and Elizabeth actually considered suicide as she wished for the death of Tommy. In reality, Elizabeth placed her life on hold so that she could more adequately, she thought, hate Tommy. After much mental and emotional torment, she realized that forgiveness held the only cure for her torment. Eventually, she forgave Tommy, restored his dignity, and came to enjoy almost a mother-son relationship with him. To heal healthily, she had to forgive. Forgiveness for both Elizabeth and for Tommy was therapeutic.[3]

THE DIVINE MODEL FOR FORGIVING

Unforgiveness can have devastating effects on our health. According to *Psychology Today*,[4] if we are still holding grudges, we need to check our pulse. New research suggests that harboring feelings of betrayal may be the cause of high blood pressure, which can ultimately lead to stroke, kidney, heart failure, and even death. The article suggests that we must either forgive or we could die. It included results of a study exploring the effects of having a forgiving personality on both psychological and physical strength responses. In the study, University of Tennessee students discussed two betrayal experiences—by a parent, friend, or romantic partner. As they spoke, researchers measured their blood pressure, heart rate, forehead muscle tension, and skin conduction response. The results, which were presented at the American Psychosomatic

Society annual meeting, showed that high forgivers (those who forgive easily), had a lower resting blood pressure rate, and smaller increases in blood pressure rates than low forgivers (those who held grudges a long time). For those who refused to forgive, the mere act of talking about the experiences caused their blood pressure to rise.

"Talking about betrayal can make anyone's blood boil," noted Kathlene Lawyer, head researcher and psychology professor at the University of Tennessee, "but forgiving transgressions appears to promote better overall health." The research further pointed out that high forgivers reported fewer physician visits for physical ailments. "Forgiveness might enhance health by reducing the excessive physiological burden that comes with unresolved stressful experiences like the hurt and offense attributed to others," Lawyer explained. "Forgiveness requires good social skills. High forgivers seem more emphatic, expressing more positive emotions towards others, including those who hurt them. Some people seem to have better life skills for maintaining satisfying relationships, and one of those skills is forgiveness. If so, then building social skills like empathy and communication may facilitate forgiveness."

Forgiveness is therapeutic. It will enhance our health. Forgiveness contributes to our psychological, physiological, and spiritual well-being. It enhances our mind, body, and spirit. Since forgiveness provides all of that, why are we so hesitant to forgive?

God forgave people so that they could be His people. Jesus modeled forgiveness for believers. He then ordered His people to forgive His people: "Be kind to one another, tender-hearted, forgiving each other, just as God in Christ also has forgiven you" (Ephesians 4:32). We ought to live lives being forgiven and forgiving. Jesus—not our mother or our father—is our model for forgiving. Not even our former way of forgiving qualifies to serve as our model for forgiving.

Most people hesitate to forgive because of the presence of false notions about the nature of forgiveness. False notions deceive us into believing that we cannot forgive. Let's look at some of the things that forgiveness is not.

1. Forgiveness is not the same as forgetting. Do we believe that if we can consciously recall how another person has violated us that we have not really forgiven? Do we believe that when we forgive we always forget? Many people say, "Oh, when you forgive, you forget"—but that is not true. God did not give us the ability to consciously erase our memories. Our intellectual capacity is powerless to intentionally erase our memories (except in the case of financial indebtedness!).

We can forgive and still remember because forgiveness and forgetting are two separate issues. Jesus talks to His disciples about forgiveness: "Then Peter came and said to Him, 'Lord, how often shall my brother sin against me and I forgive him? Up to seven times?' Jesus said to him, 'I do not say to you, up to seven times, but up to seventy times seven'" (Matthew 18:21-22).

Jesus proceeded to tell a parable of king who wished to settle accounts with his slaves. One slave, who owed him ten thousand talents, was unable to repay. He pleaded for mercy and the king felt compassion and forgave him the debt. That slave went out and found one of his fellow slaves who owed him a hundred denari. The lender slave demanded that the borrower slave pay immediately. When the borrower slave begged for mercy, the lender slave refused mercy and threw the borrower slave into prison. Word of this insensitive behavior reached the ears of the king. He summoned the lender slave (who was earlier the borrower slave) and said, "You wicked slave, I forgave you all that debt" (Matthew 18:32).

How could the king say this if forgiveness is forgetting? The king had forgiven, but he had not forgotten the amount of the debt that he had forgiven. Forgiveness and forgetting are two separate issues.

God does not erase from memory what He has forgiven. Though He had forgiven the Corinthians, God not only remembered what He had forgiven them of, but also mentioned it by inspiration to the apostle Paul. "Such were some of you" (1 Corinthians 6:11).

2. Forgiveness is not excusing the guilty from justice. Justice is moral accountability. Jesus healed the lame man who had lain at the pool of Bethesda for years (see John chapter 5). Later Jesus found the former lame man in the temple and said to him, "Behold, you have become well; do not sin anymore, so that nothing worse happens to you" (John 5:14). Jesus did not excuse the man from his behavior but rather held him accountable for his behavior. Forgiveness does not mean that justice be eliminated.

Jesus did not condemn the woman who had been caught in adultery (see John 8:1-11). Neither did he excuse her past behavior. Rather, He held her accountable for her future behavior.

3. Forgiveness is not always restoring the guilty person back to every dimension of their former relationship. Forgiveness does not always mean that we are going to have the same kind of relationship that existed before the perpetration. The father forgave his prodigal son, but reserved the inheritance posture for the older son only. The father said to his older son, "All that is mine is yours" (Luke 15:31). The younger brother who had wasted his inheritance did not enjoy the blessing of being repositioned within the will, yet he was forgiven by his father.

There are times when forgiveness may appropriate the same type of relationship as previously enjoyed, but not always. Certainly, we should not restore a relationship that was unhealthy in the first place. Forgiveness requires one changed heart while restoration demands two changed hearts. The person who is forgiven may not desire the same type relationship.

For example, one business partner discovers that her business partner has been stealing from the company. Forgiveness requires a change in the heart of the innocent partner, but to resume the partnership as it was before requires a change in the heart of the guilty party, namely, repentance.

What is forgiveness? The absence of true notions about forgiveness retards the forgiveness process.

1. Forgiveness is surrendering our right to retaliation. Retaliation frequently erupts within the family. God specifically counseled wives and husbands to avoid retaliation. "To sum up, all of you be harmonious, sympathetic, brotherly, kindhearted, and humble in spirit; not returning evil for evil or insult for insult, but giving a blessing instead" (1 Peter 3:8-9). Lust for revengeful satisfaction drives our desire to see our enemies suffer. Therefore, forgiveness is surrendering the right to retaliation. There is a difference between retaliation and discipline. Discipline seeks to rehabilitate, while retaliation seeks merely to penalize (see Hebrew 12:11).

2. Forgiveness is revising our thoughts and feelings towards the guilty. It requires that we change how we think and feel.

Jesus taught His disciples, "You have heard that it was said, 'You shall love your neighbor and hate your enemy.' But I say to you, love your enemies and pray for those who persecute you, so that you may be sons of your Father who is in heaven" (Matthew 5:43-45). This required them to revise their thoughts and feelings toward their enemy.

3. Forgiveness is rediscovering the humanity of the person who sinned against us. We have a natural tendency to reduce the perpetrator to the lowness of his crime. Instead of being our brother, he becomes nothing more than the person who violated us, that is, a thief, a murderer, etc. God told the Corinthian believers to discipline a man who seemingly was having a relationship with his father's wife, and they obeyed (see 1 Corinthians chapter 5), but to keep them from going overboard, God told the church to restore his humanity, dignity, and self-worth as an individual (see 2 Corinthians chapter 2). Certainly, the man did something inappropriate, but there is a point in time when forgiveness takes place. No longer view him as the criminal. Elevate him to the level of being a human being again.

Remember Joseph and his brothers, to whom we alluded earlier in this chapter? Because their father favored Joseph, his brothers developed a revengeful hatred for him (see Genesis chapter 37). They hated Joseph because their father treated him special. How do we feel when other people are treated special but we aren't? Always remember that a positive statement about someone else is not necessarily a negative statement about us.

The hatred of Joseph's brothers drove them to sell Joseph into slavery. This deprived Joseph of many years of family association. Thankfully, this was not the end of the story (see Genesis chapter 50). After their father died, they suspected that Joseph would seek revenge, but instead he demonstrated his forgiveness toward them.

> "As for you, you meant evil against me, but God meant it for good in order to bring about this present result, to preserve many people alive. So therefore, do not be afraid; I will provide for you and your little ones." So he comforted them and spoke kindly to them (Genesis 50:20-21).

Sounds to me as if Joseph was just bubbling over with forgiveness. After all his brothers had stolen from him, after all they had deprived him of, he readily forgave them. And not only did he forgive them, he forgave them long before they ever came and asked for it. As a matter of fact, they never really asked for forgiveness. We, too, can readily forgive even our most painful violation.

However, there is a difference between just healing and healing healthily. If we puncture our flesh with a wooden splinter and allow the splinter to remain, the flesh will grow and heal over it. Years later a cancerous sore may develop. The wound healed, but not healthily. No healthy healing takes place without forgiveness. The wound will not heal healthily until we remove the splinter. There is no healthy healing until forgiveness takes place.

Someone who has been deeply wounded—perhaps abused as a child or deserted by a spouse—might ask, "How in the world can I forgive such people? Do you understand how deep this wound is? Do you understand the emotional trauma that I have experienced for the last 30 years? Can you imagine what I have gone through? And you're telling me to forgive?"

I am saying that is the only way to heal.

How do we forgive the great hurt that was done? Let's consider some steps.

First, we must grieve our misery. Pain does serve a useful purpose. Rushing through the grieving phase may actually sabotage the healthy healing of the violation. It is appropriate to grieve; therefore, we must spend some time in the grieving phase. When we have suffered a great irretrievable loss, we may have been robbed of our innocence and our good reputation, and deprived of our family. We may have been deprived of our resources or of a fair opportunity. Whatever the situation, the hurt is deep and we need to spend some time grieving our misery.

Jacob, the grandson of the patriarch Abraham, stole the birthright from his older twin brother, Esau, and later stole his blessing (see Genesis chapter 27). In those days, the oldest son received the birthright status, which positioned him to receive a double portion of the father's inheritance. Jacob tricked his father into giving him the birthright instead of Esau.

At first, Esau was so angry that he wanted to kill his twin brother. His parents sent Jacob away for a cooling-off period. During that time, Esau forgave his brother. When they met after years of separation, Esau's behavior indicated that he had truly forgiven his brother. He ran to Jacob and kissed him giving him the ultimate social welcome (see Genesis 33:4).

While we focus on this forgiveness picture, we must not forget the earlier grieving picture. Esau forgave his brother, but his brother had never asked for forgiveness. Jacob never did anything to indicate he was sorry. Nothing. He just left. And Esau made up in his mind, "I'm going to forgive him."

Esau forgave his brother even though the pain was not over. The pain of what Esau lost to the trickery of Jacob lasted all of Esau's lifetime. It lasted into the lifetime of Esau's sons, for a blessing was generational. Even in the midst of Esau missing out on what his father would have given him—what was rightfully his—he forgave.

Imagine that. How would we react if one of our brothers cheated us out of the family inheritance? He could be living the life of luxury, drawing interest on the money, and we would not have a cent. In the midst of it all, could we forgive him? If so, it would be not just a picture of forgiveness, but a true picture of success at work.

After grieving *our* misery, it is now time to grace *His* mercy. After we have spent some time looking inward to our misery, it becomes time to look upward to His mercy. Mercy is a special and immediate regard to eliminate the misery of another. God understands when we have been mistreated, and at His appropriate time He has a special and immediate regard to eliminate our misery. He does not want us to be in misery all our life; however He will allow us to rest there for a while. Before it ever happened, God anticipated our misery and made preparations to help us through it.

> Blessed be the God and Father of our Lord Jesus Christ, the Father of mercies and God of all comfort, who comforts us in all our affliction so that we will be able to comfort those who are in any affliction with the comfort with which we ourselves are comforted by God (2 Corinthians 1:3-4).

If we have experienced a deep hurt that has not healed, these are two excellent verses to write down and put on the refrigerator, on the dashboard in the car, anywhere we can as a regular reminder that God comforts us in all afflictions. He is the God of all comfort. Every time we receive some comfort, it is from the heart of God, regardless of who it comes through, but if we continue to grieve our misery and not grace His mercy, we crowd out the God of comfort and the comfort of God.

Unforgiveness is like a flame, and we can fan the flames or put out the fire. After we have grieved our misery, at some point we must deliberately decide to stop fanning the flames and put out the fire. It is a conscious decision that we want to get beyond the shock, the denial, and the pain of what has happened. If we have lingered in resentment too long, it is time to excuse ourselves from that misery. We can talk about moving away from it, but at some point we must take the first step—and move from the misery stage to the mercy stage. There are specific ways to help us do this.

1. Find a spiritually focused confidant who has progressed beyond where we are. Such a person will ensure a therapeutic relationship, not a gossiping one. Gossip provides retaliation, but spiritual counsel brings about release. As we share our hurt with him or her, it allows God to help us heal.

2. Stop sabotaging our forgiveness ability by preprogramming ourselves to not forgive. Have we said, "If _____ happens to me, I would never forgive?" Or, "If _____

happens to me, I could never forgive?" What we say is often what we get. We must say we can and will forgive, even if we believe that we will have to struggle to do so.

3. Remember that God Himself is part of our forgiveness chain. God forgave us so that we would have a model to imitate. Those to whom Paul wrote had experienced the forgiveness of God: "Be kind to one another, tender-hearted, forgiving each other, just as God in Christ also has forgiven you" (Ephesians 4:32). With God's grace, it is possible to forgive even the worst wrong that has been done to us. It doesn't matter who did it. It doesn't matter where we were. It doesn't matter why they did it. It doesn't matter how much pain it caused us. With God's help, we can forgive.

4. Never curse our enemies. When we do, we do get even with them, but unfortunately it is at their lower level. We must not degrade ourselves to their lower level. To curse someone is not the same as using profanity, which the New Testament prohibits (see Ephesians 4:29). Cursing is much more than calling someone by a four-letter word. As a noun, a curse is God's divine sentence of destruction upon someone or something (see Mark 11:12-21 and Matthew 11:12-24). It lines up the universal forces in opposition to the well-being of another. As a verb, *to curse* means "to call, pray, and/or desire God's divine sentence of destruction upon someone or something" (see Luke 9:51-56).

God anticipated that some would say, "I may as well curse my enemies. That is the way I feel about them." He anticipated that others would say, "If I do not curse them, they will keep persecuting me." Therefore, He said, "Do not be overcome by evil, but overcome evil with good" (Romans 12:21).

6. Bless our enemies. We must speak well of—and to—those who have wounded us. Find something healthy and wholesome to say about and to them. That may seem like strange counsel, but this is what God commanded: "Bless those who persecute you; bless and do not curse" (Romans 12:14). *To persecute* literally meant to "put to flight." It meant to harass a person until that person had to run away, to drive folk away and then come after them, to resolve to make life miserable for another. Paul certainly had persecuted believers, as we read in Acts 22:4-5. He followed them in order to persecute them more (see Acts 26:9-11). In spite of his personal history, he instructed the disciples to refrain from retaliating when they encountered persecution from their enemies.

As much as truth will allow, we must speak well *to* our enemies (see Acts 5:27-32). Also, as much as truth will allow, we must speak well *of* our enemies (see Acts 7:59-60). When we bless our enemies, we do get even with them, and fortunately it is at our higher level. We must seek to elevate them to our higher level. To bless means to speak well of in order to convey favorable circumstances toward; it is to position for prosperity.

We can and should refrain from getting even with our enemies at their lower level. We can and should persist in getting even at our higher level.

7. Monitor our actions toward those who have wronged us. God's commandments in this regard are stringent:

> Never pay back evil for evil to anyone. Respect what is right in the sight of all men ... Never take your own revenge, beloved, but leave room for the wrath of God, for it is written, "Vengeance is Mine, I will repay," says the Lord. But if your enemy is hungry, feed him, and if he is thirsty, give him a drink; for in so doing you will heap burning coals on his head. Do not be overcome by evil, but overcome evil with good (Romans 12:17, 19-21).

Is He talking about the person who lied about us and caused us to lose our job? We have to feed them? Exactly.

Forgiveness is a choice. Therefore, we must deliberately choose to forgive the unforgivable. Forgiveness takes pain from the mind of the one who holds the charge. When we forgive the person who has wronged us, our mind releases them from that charge. We have the ability to forgive. God would not tell us to do something that we do not have the ability to do. Do not call God a liar. God said, "Forgive" but if we keep saying, "I cannot," we are calling Him a liar.

God decided to forgive. He made a choice. He could have decided not to forgive. Had he decided not to forgive, all humanity would have been doomed. Therefore, we forgive because God has forgiven us. "Be kind to one another, tenderhearted, forgiving each other, just as God in Christ also has forgiven you" (Ephesians 4:32). Why did God forgive us? He forgave us not because of us, but because of Jesus Christ. He forgave us not because of us, but in spite of us.

Why do we forgive? We forgive because God has forgiven us on the basis of Jesus Christ. We forgive those who have hurt us not because of them, but in spite of them. We forgive because the death, burial, and resurrection of Christ demand it. Jesus Christ was enough to cause God to forgive us. The blood of Jesus was enough to cause God to forgive us. The blood of Jesus should be enough to cause us to forgive others. If we want to be successful, we must learn to forgive. Remember, success is a God idea. So is forgiveness.

Let's write God a letter.

> *Dear God, I received a charge to forgive those who have wronged me. I learned how to take some basic steps towards forgiveness, but I have decided not to.*

Who would ever sign that letter? Our refusal to forgive signs it. Maybe we will write God another letter.

Dear God, I received a charge to forgive those who have wronged me. I learned how to take some basic steps towards forgiveness. Thank you, Lord. I will forgive.

Who will sign that letter? Our willingness to forgive is how we sign it.

John chapter 8 tells the story of the teachers of the law and the Pharisees bringing before Jesus a woman caught in the act of adultery. Right in His presence, they aired all her dirty laundry and demanded the full penalty of the law (amazingly, they let the man go). Jesus replied not with condemnation but with forgiveness. Those who are least qualified to condemn usually will, but He who is most qualified to condemn usually will not.

Let's pray to the One who refused to condemn the guilty woman but instead chose to forgive her. "God, I thank You for Your model of forgiveness. Help me to recognize where I am in the journey toward forgiveness. Help me to forgive and teach others to forgive. Bind my heart in forgiveness. Amen."

THOUGHT PROVOKERS

1. How has your concept of forgiveness changed since studying this chapter?

2. Who do you need to forgive? Where are you on the path to forgiveness—misery or mercy?

3. Are you ready to move on? What are the steps you need to take?

Chapter 10

SUCCESSFULLY CHANGING

On their evangelistic preaching expedition, Paul and Silas visited Thessalonica, a city that was both pagan and prosperous (see Acts chapter 17). Within three weeks, they had planted a thriving church there, and although their stay was short, they remembered the believers in Thessalonica for years to come. The Bible contains two letters that the apostle Paul wrote to the believers in that city: 1 Thessalonians and 2 Thessalonians. In both letters, his message centered on the theme that the Lord is coming, and that truth brought balance into the lives of the believers.

Balanced believers capture the affectionate interest of other balanced believers. Who is a balanced believer? There are certain characteristics that define them.

1. Balanced believers maintain their upward focus. Their exercise of faith is their upward focus. "[We are] constantly bearing in mind your work of faith

and labor of love and steadfastness of hope in our Lord Jesus Christ" (1 Thessalonians 1:3).

2. Balanced believers work because of their faith. "And without faith it is impossible to please Him, for he who comes to God must believe that He is and that He is a rewarder of those who seek Him" (Hebrews 11:6). Their work is a mental and/or physical activity directed toward the accomplishment of a task (see Genesis 2:5). Faith is what we do about what we believe that the Bible says.

3. Balanced believers maintain their outward focus. Their demonstration of love is their outward focus. Jesus said, "A new commandment I give to you, that you love one another, even as I have loved you, that you also love one another. By this all men will know that you are My disciples, if you have love for one another" (John 13:34-35). Labor is an exertion to the point of exhaustion, the emptying of the reserve of energy. Love is an attitude and an action that is caused by need, but regulated by relationship and resources.

> We know love by this, that He laid down His life for us; and we ought to lay down our lives for the brethren. But whoever has the world's goods, and sees his brother in

need and closes his heart against him, how does the love of God abide in him? (1 John 3:16-17).

4. Balanced believers maintain their onward focus (see 1 Thessalonians 1:3). Their remaining steadfastness of hope is their onward focus. They remain steadfast because of their hope. "In your hearts set apart Christ as Lord. Always be prepared to give an answer to everyone who asks you to give the reason for the hope that you have" (1 Peter 3:15). Steadfastness is an effort of endurance. Hope is the desire of anticipation that something will come to pass.

Balance in the life of a believer contributes to rapid church growth; imbalance retards church growth. Also, balance in the life of a believer stimulates a healthy social interaction among believers; constant imbalance may indicate that someone has never been born again. When God forgives, He gives His Holy Spirit (see Acts 2:38), and through His Holy Spirit, God brings balance into the life of believers. The Holy Spirit is God's spiritual intravenous needle, through which He injects into us His love (see Romans 5:5). Constant imbalance may indicate the absence of the Holy Spirit, which happens when someone is not a Christian. The presence of God brings balance to the life of believers.

I had the privilege of growing up with a brother who was

six years older and 100 pounds heavier than I. Our father was a strict no-nonsense disciplinarian who believed that family should coexist peacefully. He had zero tolerance for sons fighting each other. Being the pest of the two, I often irritated my brother. Being the reserved of the two, he often tolerated long periods of brotherly abuse. Occasionally, however, he attempted to even the score, and when he did I would simply run into the presence of our father. Once I got into Daddy's presence, I could peacefully walk. Never did my brother retaliate against me in the presence of our father, because he would not have allowed that.

Just as the presence of my father brought peace into the life of brothers, the presence of the heavenly Father brings balance into the lives of believers. In the presence of God, balanced believers can become changed. Balanced believers can become changed to become imitators. Paul commended the Thessalonians saying, "You also became imitators of us and of the Lord, having received the word in much tribulation with the joy of the Holy Spirit" (1 Thessalonians 1:6). Balanced believers can imitate the One who delivered the inerrant word, meaning "endowed without error." Paul and Silas delivered the inerrant word (see 1 Thessalonians 1:5, 1 Thessalonians 2:10-12, and John 16:8-15). They can imitate the One who delivered the incarnate word, meaning "endowed with a body." Jesus delivered the incarnate word (see John 1:1, 14).

Balanced believers can become not just imitators, but also illustrators. Paul said the Thessalonians "became an example to all the believers in Macedonia and in Achaia" (1 Thessalonians 1:7). Model believers can be an example to those who immediately receive the word, as did those of Macedonia (see Acts 16:9-15). In addition, model believers can also be an example to those who immediately reject the word, as did those of Achaia (see Acts 18:12-17).

We can become balanced believers and changed believers. Imitating is the way we start to change (by watching and learning from others who are where we want to be), and illustrating is the way we remain changed (by investing in others and sharing what we have learned).

To illustrate these two truths, picture Mr. and Mrs. Smith driving to dinner at the new home of some family member in another city. The directions sounded clear when the Smiths started the trip, but it isn't long before they become hopelessly lost. Two hours after circling the city looking for the elusive address, the Smiths finally give up and call their relatives, who jump into their own car and lead the Smiths right to their front door. Because Mr. Smith imitates the lead driver, he instantly changes from turning onto wrong streets to turning onto correct streets. And two months later when the Smiths return with another couple, Mr. Smith leads the way; he is now the illustrator.

Whether imitators or illustrators, balanced believers can become passionately charged about serving the Lord (see 1 Thessalonians 1:9). Saints are to become a pattern for sinners. The church is to be a pattern for the community. Faith is not just what we believe, but it is also what we do about what we believe. The Thessalonian believers turned outward to serve, and their conduct was transformed. They passionately served the Lord through their word. "The word of the Lord has sounded forth from you, not only in Macedonia and Achaia, but also in every place your faith toward God has gone forth" (1 Thessalonians 1:8). They sounded the word among those who immediately received it (see Acts 16:9) and those who immediately rejected it (see Acts 18:12).

Balanced believers can also become passionately charged about seeing the Lord. Paul commended the Thessalonians because they "turned to God from idols to serve a living and true God, and to wait for His Son from heaven, whom He raised from the dead, that is Jesus, who rescues us from the wrath to come" (1 Thessalonians 1:9-10). They turned upward to see. They trusted patiently, and their confidence was transferred from idols to the living God. They passionately waited for the Lord to come from heaven and take them to heaven. They waited to be rescued from the utter hopelessness of the wicked world that will face an angry God.

The Thessalonians did an about-face and went through a radical repentance; they successfully changed from worshiping idols to worshiping the living and true God. God's grace is available to us, also, so that we can successfully change in whatever area we need change, so that we can become balanced believers who are passionate about seeing and serving the Lord.

THOUGHT PROVOKERS

1. Who did you encounter this week who has a well-balanced spiritual life? What blessings are they enjoying? How do you feel about them and their blessings?

2. When did you last agonize with someone who seemed unable to get himself or herself together? How did you feel? What did you do?

3. How passionately charged are you about serving the Lord? About seeing the Lord?

Chapter 11

SUCCESSFULLY CHARGING BEYOND OUR PAST

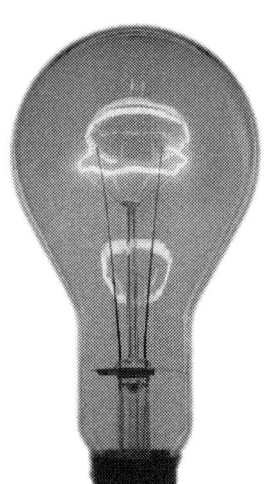

Athletes all over the world spend years preparing themselves to participate in the Olympic games. They invest all that they are and all that they have attempting to win a temporary gold medallion. For what will we invest all that we are and all that we have?

"Not that I have already obtained it or have already become perfect, but I press on so that I may lay hold of that for which also I was laid hold of by Christ Jesus" (Philippians 3:12). Christ Jesus laid hold of believers that they may lay hold of the resurrection from the dead, the ultimate goal of Christian discipleship (see Philippians 1:21, 23 and 2 Timothy 4:7-8). Through Jesus Christ, God provided an opportunity for believers to obtain a permanent prize. As Paul wrote, "I press on toward the goal for the prize of the upward call of God in Christ Jesus" (Philippians 3:14).

When he thought it through to its logical conclusion,

the apostle Paul realized that he had not obtained the ultimate goal of discipleship. "Brethren, I do not regard myself as having laid hold of it yet; but one thing I do: forgetting what lies behind and reaching forward to what lies ahead" (verse 13). Therefore, he yearned to experience the resurrection of Jesus more completely than he ever had (see verses 8-11). For him to accomplish the ultimate goal, he needed to forget the past.

Like Paul, memories of our past may limit our success. What do we need to forget? We may need to forget some of our past failures (see verse 6). When we forget our own past failures, we give ourselves another opportunity to succeed. We adopt the attitude, "I am never down, I am always up, or I am getting up." Too often we allow the ghost of our guilt—guilty feelings—to forever haunt us.

When we forget the past failures of others, we give them another opportunity to succeed. The discussion continues in an effort to answer the question, "What should we do toward those who have done evil?" This discussion stands center court in the criminal justice system. Many ex-convicts have pasts that are frightening. Some argue that we should not rehabilitate them; some believe that we cannot rehabilitate them; others believe that we must rehabilitate them. Those who say we cannot will likely point to the 1988 campaign poster of Willie Horton. While on parole, he raped a woman and stabbed her companion. Those who say we can will likely point to someone like attorney James Hamm or Dr. Paul Krueger.

James Hamm committed murder in 1974, but while in prison he transformed himself into a law-abiding scholar. After being released from prison, he graduated from college, graduated from law school, and passed the bar in Arizona—the same state that imprisoned him for more than seventeen years. In spite of his progress, some said that he was still unfit to practice law. His past still hounded his present and haunted his future. Paul Krueger, a triple murderer, ended up on the faculty at Penn State University until his criminal background was uncovered. After serving twelve years in prison, he was paroled and completed a doctorate. Even though one school administrator called him an exemplary faculty member, the murders he committed thirty-eight years earlier proved to be impossible to ignore. Like James Hamm, his past still hounded his present and haunted his future.[5]

All of us have pasts that are not only frightening, but also sinful (see Romans 3:23). How does God treat us for our past? He forgets. "For I will be merciful to their iniquities, and I will remember their sins no more" (Hebrews 8:12). How does Jesus treat us for our past? He refuses to condemn. He told a woman who was caught in the very act of adultery that He would not condemn her (see John 8:1-11).

Judas betrayed Jesus once. When Judas sought solace from the chief priest and elders, they dissociated themselves from him. Tragically his life ended in suicide (see Matthew 27:4-5). Peter denied Jesus three times. He even denounced having ever associated with Jesus (see Matthew 26:69-75). When he sought solace from the Lord, he received it. Was one betrayal worse than three denials? To focus on who committed the more grievous sin is to grossly miss the point. Peter likely believed that he could recover from his past in the future, while Judas believed that his past was the future. Because God enables us to overcome our horrendous past, let us encourage others to do so as well.

We may need to forget not just our past failures, but also our past victories (see Philippians 3:5-7). Where would the automobile industry be if it had never gone beyond the safety of seat belts to the air bag? Providing seat belts was a indicator of success for human safety, but the industry had to forget that success in order to progress to the air bag. Now automobile safety has improved even more.

In 2001, the Duke University Blue Devils basketball team, along with their coach Mike Krzyzewski, won the NCAA men's basketball championship. Some months later as they prepared for the next season, a reporter asked Coach K about his team's championship status from the past year. The insightful Coach K replied, "We are not defending our championship. We are trying to win another one." Indeed, Coach K has learned that in order to succeed we must forget even our past successes so that we can properly focus on the necessities for future successes.

When we forget our past victories, we remove the tendency to resign in order to preserve our perfect record, thereby challenging ourselves to go beyond the norm. When we forget the past victories of others, we remove their tendency to resign in order to preserve their perfect record, thereby challenging them to go beyond the norm. What if Peter had quit preaching after 3,000 people converted to Christianity on the day of Pentecost? That would have been the end of the Great Commission, and the church never would have grown beyond Jerusalem.

It is impossible, of course, to erase the memories of past victories or defeats, but we can refuse to allow them to hinder our present and/or future progress. To the extent that history helps, we ought to remember it, but to the extent that history hinders, we ought to forget it.

What are some past failures that can hinder us? Are the past failures of abortion, adultery, divorce, drug involvement, dropping out or failing in school, or homosexual encounters acting as hindrances to future success? Which past failures are we using to hinder others? We must refuse to allow anything in the past to limit us. Instead, we should seek God's forgiveness, forgive ourselves, and behave as if we are forgiven. If there is a need to forgive others, we should do so, and then treat them as if they are forgiven.

Besides forgetting the past, the apostle Paul needed to reach for the future—"forgetting what is behind and straining toward what is ahead" (Philippians 3:13 NIV). His words describe an athlete running at top speed and straining his entire body to cross the finish line ahead of the other runners. Yet while running, he remained on course, refusing to allow anything to cause him to swerve off course. This is the same drive and focus that Nehemiah had (see Nehemiah 6:1-4). Reaching for the future develops an attitude that says, "Today is the first day of the rest of my life." Focusing on the future will sustain our spiritual momentum.

As we successfully charge beyond our past, we should focus individually and collectively. Individually, we strain toward the finish line, yet remain on course. We must focus our thoughts, words, and actions toward the goal. Collectively, we strive toward the finish line with others. It is good to bring someone along with us; they challenge us and we challenge them, and together we focus our thinking, talking, and travel toward the goal. We go for the gold; we go for the goal.

THOUGHT PROVOKERS

1. If you stand on the right track but do not move, will you go anywhere? Is there a chance you will be run over?

2. What vision has God given you for the future? What do you need to leave behind from the past in order to charge into the future?

3. Are you willing to allocate 60 seconds each morning to think about your goals and say them aloud, and then do something positive about your goals every day? When will you begin?

Chapter 12

SUCCESSFULLY PERSUADING UNBELIEVERS TO BELIEVE

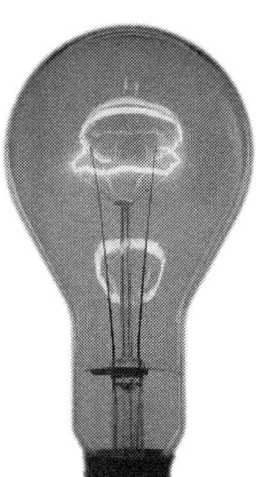

The timekeeper at the basketball game forgot that he was the timekeeper, and got so caught up watching the game that he became a spectator. He failed to promptly start the clock. He forgot who he was.

Before leaving home, parents say to their children, "Do not forget who you are." Remembering who we are helps us to remember how we are supposed to behave.

It is vital to remember who we are and what we are supposed to be doing. Apollos and Paul remembered who they were; they were believing servants. They also remembered what they were supposed to be doing: Believing servants persuaded unbelievers to believe. Everywhere they went throughout the book of Acts, they persuaded unbelievers to believe. Even in Corinth, they persuaded people to believe that Jesus was the Christ, the Son of God (see Acts 18:4 and 1 Corinthians 3:5).

At our conversion, our Lord instilled in us a natural desire to lead others to Christ. As soon as Andrew believed in Jesus, "The first thing Andrew did was to find his brother Simon and tell him, 'We have found the Messiah'" (John 1:40 NIV). As soon as Philip heard, he found Nathanael and told him (see verse 45). This ministry to reconcile the world to Christ is given to all believers at the time of their new birth:

> If anyone is in Christ, he is a new creature; the old things passed away; behold, new things have come. Now all these things are from God, who reconciled us to Himself through Christ and gave us the ministry of reconciliation, namely, that God was in Christ reconciling the world to Himself, not counting their trespasses against them, and He has committed to us the word of reconciliation. Therefore, we are ambassadors for Christ, as though God were making an appeal through us (2 Corinthians 5:17-20).

This is part of our genetic make-up as believers, but ridiculing unbelievers and reluctant believers have suppressed our natural desire. Many unbelievers live in our community. Some live down the street, next door, and even in the same house with us. We must persuade unbelievers to believe that Jesus is the Christ, the Son of God, and God will help us be successful at doing so.

Why should we persuade unbelievers to believe? Because "we are God's fellow workers" (1 Corinthians 3:9). The word *we* in this verse refers specifically to Paul and Apollos, but of course it also refers to all believers (see verse 5). The word *are* refers to our current status. *Workers* refers to those who work; what is the work to which God has called us? Paul says, "The Lord has assigned to each his task" (verse 5 NIV). What is our task? What are we supposed to be doing?

Paul continues, "I planted the seed, Apollos watered it, but God made it grow" (verse 6 NIV). If there is no belief growing in the hearts of some, perhaps it is because we have not planted a seed of belief there—precisely placing the word of God into the hearts of unbelievers (see Luke 8:11). Or perhaps we have not watered the seed that another planted—purposefully encouraging those who have heard the word. A pineapple will not grow in Decatur, Georgia, because the climate is not right; it discourages pineapple growth. Why is there no belief growing in the hearts of some? Often we have not provided a climate that encourages growth.

We should persuade unbelievers to believe because we are God's fellow workers. We must abandon individual agendas, and actively cooperate and participate with God.

> So neither he who plants nor he who waters is
> anything, but only God, who makes things grow.
> The man who plants and the man who waters

have one purpose, and each will be rewarded according to his own labor. For we are God's fellow workers; you are God's field, God's building (1 Corinthians 3:7-9 NIV).

God tells us what to teach and what seeds to plant (see Matthew 28:18-20). Jesus never allowed His apostles to invent their own message; they taught His message (see John 16:12-13). He also tells us how to teach and water the seeds (see Ephesians 4:15), and how to convince others that Jesus is the Christ, the Son of the living God. We might say, "I cannot persuade people," but we can. Within our natural circle of influence, we can simply and easily tell people what Jesus has done (see John 4:28-29). God will help us to become successful at convincing unbelievers to believe in Him.

After Paul was converted, God used him to convert people every year. Through us, God will convert at least one person per year. He will start when we see the vision, just as Paul saw the vision:

> During the night Paul had a vision of a man of Macedonia standing and begging him, "Come over to Macedonia and help us." After Paul had seen the vision, we got ready at once to leave for Macedonia, concluding that God had called us to preach the gospel to them (Acts 16:9-10 NIV).

That vision ignited Paul, and it enabled him to be a successful soul winner. A vision is a mental picture. For example, we explain an idea and then ask, "Do you see what I am saying?"

Observe the petition of Paul's vision: "Come…and help us" (verse 9 NIV). Today, many are begging to be taught. When they admit their human inadequacies, they are asking us to help them access divine help. Observe the posture of the vision; the man from Macedonia was standing, which symbolized the urgent need. Today the need is even more urgent.

Observe the timing of the visit. They prepared at once (see verse 10) and went while hearts remained receptive. Many souls are lost through delay that allows Satan another opportunity to disinterest potential converts. Observe the togetherness of the visit (see verse 10). The evangelist saw the vision, but others went. They understood that through the vision of one, God reaches and rewards many; therefore, they didn't say, "Paul, it was your vision, so you go" (see Matthew 10:40-41). Observe the fruit of the victory (see Acts 16:14-15). Forgiveness of sins was a fruit of this victory. Observe the follow-up of the victory (see verses 16-39).

Through us, God will convert at least one person per year when we make the effort to go to those around us and speak.

Earlier, we looked at 2 Corinthians 5:18. "God…reconciled us to Himself through Christ and gave us the ministry of reconciliation." Through Jesus Christ, God reconciled sinners to Himself. *To reconcile* means "to reestablish a favorable relationship." Through Jesus Christ, God reestablished a favorable relationship with those who would become born again, but He did not stop there (although many of us do). To those whom He had reconciled, God gave the ministry of reconciliation. He gave them the opportunity to participate in His reestablishing favorable relationships with others. Reconciled saints inform unreconciled sinners that the way to God leads through Jesus Christ (see Acts 8:4).

God gave to the apostle Paul the ministry of reconciliation. Through the preaching of the cross, the apostle Paul persuaded and begged people to be reconciled to God (see 2 Corinthians 5:11, 20 and 1 Corinthians 1:18-23). Yes, he exercised his ministry gift of reconciliation.

How do we feel when people do not use the gifts that we have given them? How does God feel when we do not use the gifts that He has given us? What is the least-used gift that God has given us? Very likely it is the gift of the ministry of reconciliation. How do we use this wonderful gift?

Inform people that God took their sin and credited them to Christ's account (see 2 Corinthians 5:21). God debited their account and credited the account of Jesus. Therefore, when God looks at them, He sees only the sinlessness of Jesus.

Inform people that God took the righteousness of Jesus and credited it to their account. God credited their account with righteousness, and debited the account of Jesus. Therefore, when God looks at us, He sees only the righteousness of Jesus.

Share the news of the availability of salvation that is found only in Christ Jesus. Reconciliation was accomplished at the cross, but it is appropriated at conversion. University school loans for the year are accomplished when approved, but appropriated at the beginning of each semester. Our earnings are accomplished each hour, but appropriated when we cash our paycheck.

Tell people that God longs to take their sins and credit them to Jesus' account and credit to their account the righteousness of Jesus.

Perhaps you have never opened your gift of reconciliation. Perhaps it has sat, still wrapped, in a dark closet since the day you were saved. Now is the time to unwrap it and put it to use. If you need more direction, ask the Lord to show you how to be a successful soul winner. Remember, success is His idea, and He will joyfully partner with you as you introduce others to Him.

THOUGHT PROVOKERS

1. What challenges you in this chapter to become more successful at persuading unbelievers to believe?

2. When was the last time you used your gift of reconciliation? Are you pleased with that time frame?

3. What is your role in evangelism? What is God's role? How can you work together?

Chapter 13

YOU CAN BE A SUCCESS!

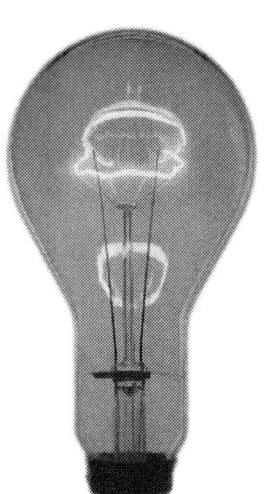

I learned a lot about success from my parents, Cleveland and Annie Sue Boyd Marshall. My mother lived six decades without learning to drive. Occasionally my father served as her taxi, but mostly she depended on me for her mobility. In 1975, I enlisted in the U. S. Air Force and discussed selling my car. Daddy suggested (jokingly, I think) that I teach Mother how to drive. Because she knew that her traveling would be seriously curtailed when I left, she stood up to the challenge. Daily, I would back the car into the driveway, and at her leisure she would drive around the community and return the car to the driveway.

After driving without incident, she decided to take the driver's license test. I took her to the examination station and she passed the written test with flying colors. The patrolman came outside for the driving test, and asked my mother to back the car alongside the curb so that he could get in. I felt as if a ton of bricks had fallen on my head because I realized

I had taught Mother how to drive forward, but not one time had I taught her how to back up.

My mother got into the car and immediately backed up—right onto the curb. The patrolman was very cordial and allowed her to proceed with the road test. When they returned, he stated that he had to fail her, but he had allowed her to proceed so that he would not discourage her.

Within the next month, she failed the road test five times. On the sixth attempt, she succeeded in passing the road test and obtained her driver license. For the past twenty-nine years, she has been safely driving. Praise the Lord, she has never had a serious accident. Soon to be eighty-nine years young, she drives eighty miles to Memphis on Interstate 40 whenever she wants to.

Success never flows in a vacuum. You must learn the principles and follow them diligently. Just as God challenged Joshua, you too must give great care to follow success principles. Remember our definition of success? It is a healthy progression toward a predetermined wholesome goal, or the healthy progression away from an unwholesome environment. Recall that there can be no real success without dedication to God. We have looked at the lives of Abraham, Joseph, Moses, Joshua, the Israelites, King David, King Solomon, Nehemiah, Jesus, the disciples of Jesus, Lydia, the Macedonians, and others. Their success grew on the basis of their dedication to

God. That is because our success is not about us but about God.

The Bible says that God gloriously rejoices when a sinner repents (see Luke 15:7). God has granted me—a repentant sinner—the privilege to minister His word by speaking (television) and writing (books). Many have repented and turned to God. That gives Him glory. My success is not about me, but about God.

Remember Katherine, the factory worker? Her success was not just about her. Her job enabled her to help provide for her family. Providing for one's family gives God His glory.

And do not forget about my mother. Her driving success was not just about her skill as a driver nor my skill as an instructor. God has been glorified by her driving. She has made countless trips to visit those who were sick. She has catered to the needs of those who needed help. Regularly she spends her day transporting elderly ladies to the grocery store for their monthly shopping. She even drove Daddy to the emergency room when he became ill. Through all of this, God gets His glory. Do set out on your success journey, but before you take one step, decide how you will use the success that you achieve to express your dedication to God and give Him His glory and honor.

I am not the only one who has worked forty hours per week

and succeeded academically. God has done this for many, and He will again. He will do it for you. For you, with you, and through you, He will perform some awesome feats. He invites you to recline at ringside while He corrals His foes and to stand in the stadium while He champions His friends. With a great and awesome God like this, you cannot help but succeed.

You can and you must succeed. The generation preceding you demands it. Those who have already walked the historical halls of success are beckoning you to come. The past deserves your success. You cannot fail them.

You can and you must succeed. The generation presently with you demands it. Those who are now walking the halls of success desire and depend on your company. The present desires your success. You cannot fail them.

You can and you must succeed. The generation that will follow you demands it. Those who are waiting to walk the halls of success need role models and motivators. The future needs your success. You cannot fail them.

Yes, God Himself waits for your success. The heavenly chorus has assembled. The archangel has stood to direct the production. All of glory is waiting for you to take your seat. Do come now and let the celebration begin. Heaven needs your success. You cannot fail them.

God is with you. He wants you to succeed. Therefore, you cannot excuse yourself from the challenge. Do not surrender. At best, succeed; at worst, die trying. God wants you, helps you, and rejoices when you succeed.

Appreciate and appropriate the principles of this book. Enjoy the success that it brings. Tell others about God. Tell others about your success. Tell others about this book. Start telling others about your book. Yes, keep the success flowing.

After all, success is not just a good idea. Success is a God idea.

ENDNOTES

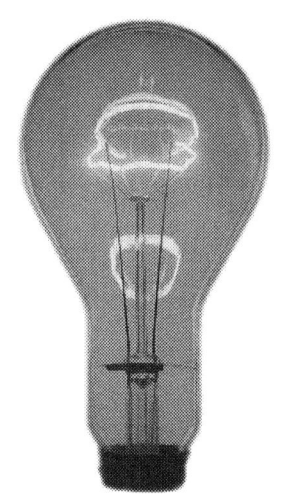

[1] *Talking Straight*, by Lee Iacocca (Bantam, 1988)

[2] *Single-mothering Stimulates a Positive Family Networking Within Black Families*, written by John Marshall for "Seminar on the Family" course, with Dr. Roger Bates, instructor, Memphis State University, 1991. This paper was one of three selected to be presented at the Graduate Symposium. Sources referenced in the excerpt: Billingsley, Andrew, 1973, "Black family structure: myths and realities," *Social Forces* 67:715-29; Chatters, Linda M., Robert Joseph Taylor, and Harold W. Neighbors, 1989, "Size of informal helpers network mobilized during a serious personal problem among Black Americans," *Journal of Marriage and the Family* 51:667-76; Garfinkel, Irwin, 1986, "Single mothers and their children: an American dilemma," *Social Forces* 68:797-812; Gibson, Rose, 1982, "Blacks at middle and later life: resources and coping," *Annals of the American Academy of Political and Social Science* 46:79-90; Hogan, Dennis P., 1990, "Race, kin, networks and assistance to mother-headed families," *Social Forces* 68:797-812; McAdoo, Harriette, 1978, "Factors related to stability in upward mobile Black families," *Journal of Marriage and the Family* 40:761-76

3 "Could They Forgive Their Son's Killer," *Reader's Digest*, May 1986

4 "Forgive," *Psychology Today*, July/August 2000

5 "Murder's Stain: Can It Be Erased?" by Milan Simonich, *Pittsburgh Post-Gazette*, August 10, 2003 (www.post-gazette.com/pg/03222/210010.stm)

OTHER BOOKS BY JOHN MARSHALL

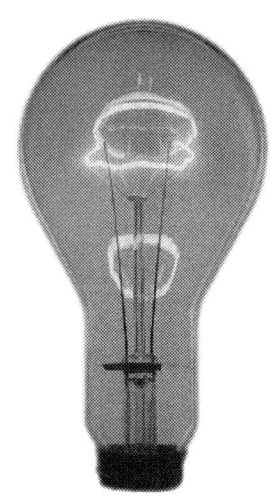

Final Answer:
You Asked, God Answered

Good and Angry
A Personal Guide to Anger Management

God Knows!
There Is No Need to Worry

God, Listen!
Prayers That God Always Answers
(includes addiction-recovery guide)

My God !
Who He Is Will Change Your Life

The Power of the Tongue
What You Say Is What You Get

Show Me the Money
7 Exercises That Build Economic Strength

ABOUT THE AUTHOR

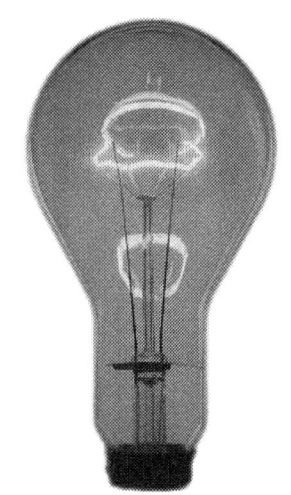

John Marshall has given more than 2,000 presentations throughout the United States, helping thousands of people with his practical and penetrating teaching style. He is an author, editor, media producer, facilitator for conflict resolution, motivational speaker, preacher, public relations director, teacher, trainer, and relationship consultant. He received his bachelor's degree from Freed-Hardeman University, master's degree in counseling from Theological University of America, and has done additional graduate work at University of Memphis and Southern Christian University. He is a staff writer for *The Christian Echo* and *The Revivalist* magazine, a member of the Alumni Advisory Board of Freed-Hardeman University, and preaches for Graceview Church of Christ in Stone Mountain, Georgia, where he and his family live.

CONTACT INFORMATION

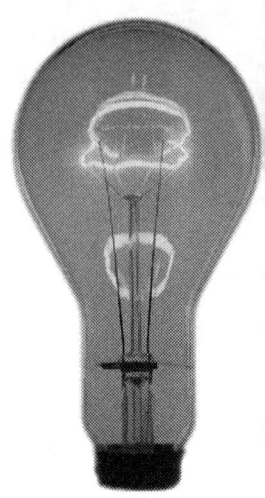

For further information about John Marshall, his ministry, and other ministry resources, please contact him at

Mail:
John Marshall
P. O. Box 878
Pine Lake Georgia 30072

Web:
www.graceview.us

Email:
jdm@graceview.us

Phone:
(404) 297-9050
(404) 316-5525

www.ingramcontent.com/pod-product-compliance
Lightning Source LLC
Chambersburg PA
CBHW051438290426
44109CB00016B/1607